T0299272

Halal Supply Chain Integrity

The market and demand for halal goods and services is ever increasing, and, with it, the importance of supply chain integrity also increases. Integrity, from the perspective of halal logistics service providers, is a prerequisite of halal compliance. This book provides a unique overview of halal supply chain integrity (HSCI) using examples from Malaysia country as a case.

The book carefully addresses and simplifies the issues of integrity in halal logistics and supply chain. It gathers findings from studies on halal supply chain integrity conducted in Malaysia, a leading country in halal production, to shed light on current issues, developments and future trends on the theory and practice of halal in the logistics sector. The book discusses factors such as halal quality assurance, trust and commitment and halal assets specificity, in particular.

This book will be a useful reference to research scholars and professionals who wish to understand halal logistics and supply chain management and also the importance of protecting integrity of halal services and products.

Zawiah Abdul Majid is a Senior Lecturer and Head of Teknoputra, International, Industrial & Institutional partnerships (3IP), at the Universiti Kuala Lumpur, Malaysia.

Mohd Farid Shamsudin is an Associate Professor at the Universiti of Kuala Lumpur, Malaysia.

Nor Aida Abdul Rahman is an Associate Professor and Head of Aviation Management at the Universiti of Kuala Lumpur, Malaysia.

Halal Supply Chain Integrity

Concept, Constituents and Consequences

**Zawiah Abdul Majid,
Mohd Farid Shamsudin and
Nor Aida Abdul Rahman**

Routledge
Taylor & Francis Group

LONDON AND NEW YORK

First published 2023
by Routledge
4 Park Square, Milton Park, Abingdon, Oxon OX14 4RN

and by Routledge
605 Third Avenue, New York, NY 10158

Routledge is an imprint of the Taylor & Francis Group, an informa business

British Library Cataloguing-in-Publication Data
A catalogue record for this book is available from the British Library

Library of Congress Cataloging-in-Publication Data
A catalog record has been requested for this book

ISBN: 978-1-032-30556-1 (hbk)
ISBN: 978-1-032-30558-5 (pbk)
ISBN: 978-1-003-30568-2 (ebk)

DOI: 10.4324/9781003305682

Typeset in Times New Roman
by codeMantra

Contents

Figures

Tables

Introduction

The emergence of halal logistics and halal supply chain (HSC) has attracted many scholars and practitioners to explore further in this area to improve current practices in handling halal products. Since 2010, halal study, in particular, halal logistics and supply chain, has gained popularity and become a potential area of research.

This book is unique in providing a composite overview of halal in logistics and supply chain areas by focusing on halal integrity throughout the HSC process. Integrity, from the perspective of halal logistics service providers (HLSP), is a prerequisite of halal compliance. Halal integrity in managing the food supply chain from producers to consumers has become more challenging. HSC is similar to the conventional supply chain, but it only caters to halal-certified products, from production to the consumption point. The concern about halal integrity is a crucial and significant challenge to maintain halal compliances. Therefore, halal traceability, halal quality assurance, halal assets specificity, trust and commitment are determining factors of effectiveness and efficiency of HLSP in halal supply chain integrity (HSCI). This research aims to measure the relationship of halal quality assurance, halal assets specificity and trust toward HSCI with commitment as mediator and barriers as moderator.

This study is unique on its own as it will provide a holistic definition of halal logistics, HSC management, halal integrity and HSCI. This book will be the main reference to readers in the logistics and supply chain field, as well as in marketing and logistics, distribution and management. This book also highlights case studies on HSCI performed in Malaysia and provides a detailed explanation of the study by using a quantitative research method, which focuses on halal logistic service providers. Six hundred questionnaires were distributed among halal logistics providers. The result of data collection indicate only 67% response rate. Data were analysed using SPSS and SmartPLS.

DOI: 10.4324/9781003305682-1

The findings revealed that asset specificity and quality assurance were not significant towards HSCI, and quality assurance was not found to be positively related to commitments. It is also interesting to know that barriers did not significantly influence the relationship between commitments and HSCI. The findings of this study would give some insights into the HLSP in Malaysia and internationally.

This Routledge focus book provides groundbreaking research on HSCI, case study application, theoretical discussion, as well as discussion on HSCI Concept, Constituents and Consequences (3Cs). This book is very special as it gathers findings from HSCI studies conducted in a leading country in halal production namely Malaysia. Readers, scholars or practitioners from other countries in the West, neighbouring Asia and Middle East are also allowed to expose and access the information with regard to halal logistics and supply chain on current issue and development, future trends, international issue, international trends, theory and practice of halal in the logistics sector.

This book will be a valuable source for readers as it provides basic and advanced concepts of halal logistics and supply chain management based on the Malaysian case studies on HSCI. The main questionnaires provided in the Appendix section will also be the main reference for scholars to continue this study in different contexts in future.

This book carefully addresses, unifies and simplifies the 'integrity' issues in halal logistics and supply chain by bringing together the expertise of academics and practitioners with extensive experience in this field. This book is also suitable for the public, regulators and other industry experts interested in this field.

Organization of the Book

After this introduction, Part I provides a detailed explanation of halal concept, as well as the evolution of halal market, halal business and the need for HSCI. It highlights the important aspects pertaining to halal logistics and supply chain, provides key evolution of halal logistics and explains how it is different from conventional logistics supply chain activities. At the same time, this part also aims to elaborate on key development and issues pertaining to halal logistics throughout the supply chain, especially in handling (transportation & warehousing activities) halal product activities. Chapter 1 provides the reader with the basic knowledge about maintaining halal integrity (assurance of halal status) throughout the supply chain, which connects to upholding integrity of the halal status from one point to another point through the supply chain network, from production to consumption. This book continues with explanation on the halal concept and the Islamic principles.

In Part II, the authors discuss the key elements of halal integrity in assuring the status of halal products throughout the supply chain and highlight the main results from case studies performed in Malaysia. Malaysia is chosen in this research as it is known as a leading or pioneer country in the halal industry and aims to become a global halal hub of the world. The study results confirm that four key variables, namely halal assets specificity, halal quality assurance, trust and commitments, significantly affect halal integrity in supply chain. Case studies conducted in Malaysia used a positivist quantitative approach with a questionnaire survey as the main method for data collection. There are 130 respondents from HLSP involved in this study. The analysis was performed using structural equation modelling, partial lease square (SEM PLS).

In Part III, the authors highlight the key contribution of the study on HSCI, and how the study contributes to the theory, industry/ practitioners, public and to the halal regulators. In this chapter, the author also provides a few suggestions for future research avenues. This study also discusses how the current outcome from this case study could be extended to other halal neighbouring countries such as Singapore, Brunei, Indonesia, Thailand, Korea, Vietnam, India, China, and Spain. The discussion is not only limited to halal practice countries or Islamic countries, but also to non-Islamic countries, especially in the western context such as Europe, the United Kingdom, Ocean region and the United States.

Part I

Halal Concept and the Overview of Halal Supply Chain Integrity

1 Halal Concepts

Halal is an Arabic term that explains two main components namely permissible (allowed by Islamic law/shariah principles) and thayyib (cleanliness). Halal has been clearly explained in four surah in Quran namely surah Al-Baqarah, An-Nahl, Al-Maidah and Al-Anfals. The term haram is opposite to halal, and it refers to any prohibited item and actions not allowed in Islamic law. Specifically, the life of every Muslim is to be guided by Shariah (Islamic Law). The Islamic law is based on four references namely Quran (The Holy Book), Hadith (sayings of the Prophet), Ijma' (consensus of the scholars) and Hadith (sayings of the Prophet).

Essentially, halal can be viewed from three generic perspectives: from a religious point of view, business point of view and scholars view (Figure 1.1). Halal in religious point of view refers to an obligation that should be fulfilled by all Muslims. While from business point of view, it refers to a good business opportunity at a global or international halal market. Halal is acknowledged as a major breakthrough and opens big opportunity for many industry players in many sectors; it has become a trend for many businesses to go for halal certification

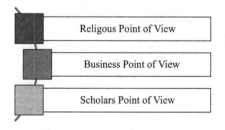

Figure 1.1 Halal view
Source: The authors

DOI: 10.4324/9781003305682-3

and to get halal logo to ensure their product is marketable and sellable. Many people believe in halal products as they are recognized as properly prepared and clean. Halal branding has been established to align with the development of halal products and services.

Because of the enhancement of halal market, business and operation, there is need for extensive research to further improve the halal practice along the supply chain to preserve the halal status of halal products. With this objective, the word halal integrity is introduced, which insists on the assurance of the halal status of halal products throughout the supply chain. While in the service context, it is also significant to have halal management systems to preserve halal integrity.

To have a clearer understanding of the concept of halal in supply chain, the next section will discuss the halal market overview and the evolution of halal logistics and supply chain. It is important to note that halal integrity is not only about the ingredients or sources of the products but also about the handling process in supply chain activity. This includes every handling process throughout the supply chain including the transportation of the halal products, storage and warehouse of the halal products, also at the retail (Rahman et al., 2014, 2018). The main aim is to ensure there is no cross-contamination happened throughout the supply chain activity from the point of production to the point of consumption by consumers.

2 Market Overview, Evolution of Halal Market and Halal Supply Chain

In championing the world's halal growth, Malaysia has presented a massive opportunity for the world economies. Malaysian halal industry has contributed approximately 7.5% to the country's GDP. Over 7,400 companies are halal-registered, generating 249,000 jobs. Over 1,700 of these companies actively export to regional and overseas markets. The number of halal exporters reported in 2019 was 1,876, and it was around 1,827 in 2018, representing a 2.7% increment in growth (Department of Statistics Malaysia, 2020). The majority of these Malaysian exporters are represented by 1,430 small and medium-sized companies, contributed to 75% of the total size, whereas the balance exporters are the MNCs. Malaysia's annual halal exports were estimated to be RM50 Billion forecasted in 2020.

Malaysia's economy was projected to expand 4.6% in 2021 and expected to achieve high-income country status by 2024. The world population is expected to increase, with the projected number double to 3 Billion by 2060 (World Population Review, 2020). The global Muslim population is expected to increase by 27% in 2050, with an estimated consumption of over USD15 trillion on halal products (Thurasamy et al., 2019). The global halal food market value reached US$1.6 trillion in 2018. Therefore, to move forward, the market value is projected US$2.9 trillion by 2024, exhibiting a CAGR of 11% between 2019 and 2024 (Dubai International Financial Centre, 2018).

The economy expected from halal industry growth is a reflection of a steady establishment of halal economy over the years, primarily driven by a large, young and fast-growing global Muslim demographic in the global economic system. Malaysia ranks 12th position among the 190 economies worldwide, a further improvement from the 15th position in 2019 as reported by the World Bank Doing Business 2020 (MITI, 2019). Considering the halal food/product potential, Malaysia aims to become the leading player for halal production, marketing,

DOI: 10.4324/9781003305682-4

certification and a halal industry reference point. The halal industry master plan 2030 shows that the halal industry is becoming important to the country's economy (Figure 2.1).

Business opportunities in the halal industry are estimated to be over 70% of Malaysia's exports, Food and Beverage (F&B) and ingredients (Fauzi et al., 2020). Such a vast potential market should be good enough to encourage local producers' capacity and capability to increase the volume and value of halal products exportation. They are attracting investment from big brands, multinational companies (MNCs) and large local companies (LLCs) to leapfrog the halal industry. MNCs have the advantage of the government incentive to make Malaysia their halal production centre and benefit the local companies through customer and supplier relationships. Figure 2.2 indicates the halal strategy and ecosystem.

The Notion of Halal Logistics and Supply Chain

At present, more companies in the halal food industry have contributed to the Islamic economy as more products are increasingly halal

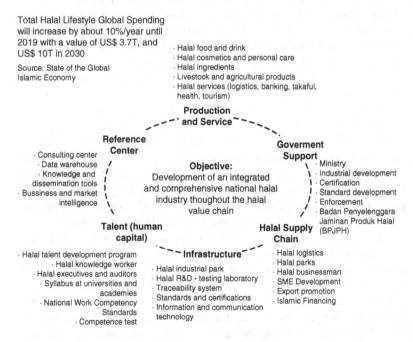

Figure 2.1 Halal industry master plan 2030 in Malaysia country

Notable Agenda:

- Malaysia
  - Global Halal Hub
    - Standard Development
    - Halal Parks
    - Talent Development & Research
- Turkey: Global Standard : SMIIC (OIC)
- UAE
  - Economic Zone, Logistic & Hubs
- Saudi Arabia
  - World's Largest Knowledge City
- Far East: Japan, China
  - Halal Cuisine
  - Japan Olympic (Halal Friendly)
- China: Halal Tourism & Trade Centres
- Thailand: Halal Research
  Private Initiatives: Zilzar (B2C, B2B), GHDP (GS1-Halal)

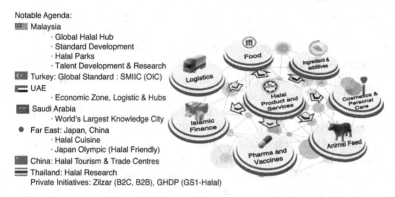

Figure 2.2 The growth of halal eco-system
Source: Halalindustryquest.com, 2016

certified. Portfolio diversification of the company increased to cater to regulatory oversight of Halal food production. The growing spending of Muslims on food and beverages increased to 6.1% and is expected in 2023 forecast to reach US$1.9 trillion. Such a result is a significant opportunity and massive investment in the creation of halal food brands globally. Therefore, one of the essential elements of ensuring halal food for consumables is practicing the halal supply chain (HSC).

Based on HSC, integrity from halal logistics service providers (HLSP) is a prerequisite as globalization increases the complexity of upholding halal integrity in managing the food supply chain from producers to consumers. According to Zulfakar et al. (2012), HSC is similar to the conventional supply chain, which comprises planning, implementing and controlling distribution and storage. However, it only caters to halal-certified products, from production to the consumption point. The concern on halal integrity is a crucial and significant challenge to maintain this halal performance. HLSP could guarantee halal integrity, along with halal supply chain activities, only for those under their supervision. Therefore, halal traceability, halal quality assurance, halal assets specificity, trust and commitment are essential factors in determining the effectiveness and efficiency of HLSP in HSC integrity.

Moving from Conventional Logistics Service Provider (LSP) to HLSP

In general, halal logistics refer to a process of planning, implementing and managing the efficient, seamless flow and storage of halal-certified products (raw materials, semi-finished or finished good) from production to the final consumption ensuring full Syariah compliance. While LSP is a company that provides management over the flow of goods and materials between the point of origin to end-use destination. The provider will often handle shipping inventory, warehousing, packaging and security functions for shipments.

The role of HLSP is very crucial in assuring halal integrity in supply chain management. Having better understanding of the roles and challenges of HLSP especially in handling halal food or product is a prerequisite for ensuring Shariah and halal laws compliance. HLSP activity at each point of supply chain activity must adhere to halal logistics management system guideline, which is in line with Shariah compliance. It is important to ensure that the integrity of halal product is safeguarded. It is the role of HLSP to carefully consider every aspect of the management system in their logistics activity, especially during transportation and at the warehouse, to avoid contamination of products with non-halal or haram substances.

Process of planning, implementing and managing the efficient, seamless flow and storage of halal-certified products (raw materials, semi-finished or finished good) from the origin to the final consumption ensuring full Syariah compliance." Certified Malaysia Halal Logistics Standard: MS2400–1–2010 Distribution, MS2400–2–2010 Warehousing & MS2400–3–2010 Retailing (DSM., 2010).

According to Zulfakar et al. (2012), halal logistics avoids contamination of perishable raw materials and food products while transporting or distributing halal products. Research by H.A. Tarmizi et al. (2014) claims that halal logistics applies the same principles as conventional logistics, but with a special exception on the type of products handled. Halal logistics is an enabler in the HSC that distributes halal products from the source to consumption without breaking the chain. Generally, halal logistics are engaged with three main elements: transportation, terminal operation and warehouse.

Halal logistics has been defined as "the process of managing the procurement, movement, storage, and handling of materials, parts, livestock, semi-finished or finished inventory both food and non-food, and related information and documentation flows through the organization and the supply chain in compliance with the general principles of Shariah'" The logistics of halal products are doubtful and questionable by the food industry and the logistics industry, therefore, exploring halal logistics along the supply chain is desirable, initiatives toward Halal standard is highly recommendable, Muhammad et al. (2009), Othman et al. (2009), Abdul et al. (2009).

Academic research on halal logistics is required as it is a new area in supply chain management. The introduction of halal logistics is the result of innovation in logistics, which does not contradict the Shariah law (Al-Salem, 2009; Zakaria, 2008; Laldin, 2006). The principles and foundation of the halal logistics are for Muslim and Non-Muslim countries. Halal logistics activities include warehousing, transportation and terminal operation. According to Tieman (2013), Halal logistics requires extensive research addressing the definition, procedures and process, including tracking and tracing, corrective measure, packaging and labelling and certification.

Halal is extending towards logistics; the findings of halal control and assurance in the logistics of halal food show that product characteristics (bulk versus unitized, ambient versus a cool chain) and market requirements (Muslim versus non-Muslim country) influence the vulnerability of halal supply chains (Ab Talib et al., 2016; Ahmad & Shariff, 2016; Fathi et al., 2016). Vulnerability is reduced by establishing halal control activities and assurance activities in logistics business processes. Vulnerability can be avoided in (parts of) the supply chain by having dedicated logistics infrastructure, like a dedicated halal warehouse and designated transport, or through containerization at a lower level. The proposed halal assurance system can be an important instrument in organizing halal food chains' logistics in Muslim and non-Muslim countries (Tieman and Ghazali, 2014). Halal assurance system (HAS) is an important aspect that needs to be considered when logistics companies are involved in the halal sector.

In Malaysia, for example, there is a standard guideline for HLSP to successfully implement halal logistics services, and the standard is known as MS2400. This halal logistics standard is a document developed by Standards Department of Malaysia in 2010. It is developed to address issues in Halal supply chain management, such as how to ensure halal assurance from farm to fork when it is being transported, and when it is being stored. Essentially, there are three main objectives of MS2400 development: First is to assure the products transports and storage at the warehouse are in accordance with halal requirements; the second is to ensure that the physical contact between halal and non-halal or with haram substance is not occurring during transportation and warehousing activity And the third is to preserve halal integrity of the product during transportation and warehousing activity.

As mentioned earlier, Halal is not only about permissible, but also clean and wholesome to be used or consumed. Hence, the participation of Halal logistics service provider (HLSP) in each supply chain activity is critical to ensure the status of Halal product that they

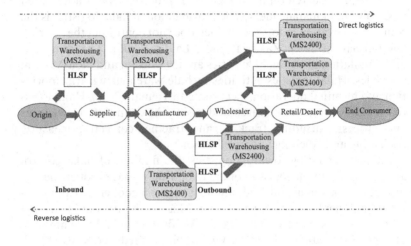

Figure 2.3 The role of HLSP along the supply chain network
Source: Rahman et al., 2020

carry throughout the supply chain is still Halal when it reach final destination. The role of HLSP activity in supply chain network is explained in Figure 2.3, and it shows the two main activities by HLSP namely transportation and warehousing. This activity is a key activity for HLSP for both inbound and outbound activity, as well as for both direct and reverse logistics activity.

What Is Halal Supply Chain Integrity (HSCI) and Why Is It Important?

The increase of halal integrity awareness in supply chain has created high demand in terms of knowledge and practical solutions. The coverage of halal integrity in supply chain is wide and crucial to have a better understanding of Halal integrity philosophy. The questions now, how can one upholding the halal integrity in ensuring the "Halalness" of the product is guaranteed?

Based on that, the knowledge of halal integrity definition should be given an extra attention to avoid any confusion. Integration and collaboration among halal stakeholder are prerequisite in determining potential business growth for sustainability. Figure 2.4 sheds light on the various definition of integrity precisely. It is significant to comprehend the meaning of halal integrity in relation to halal supply chain.

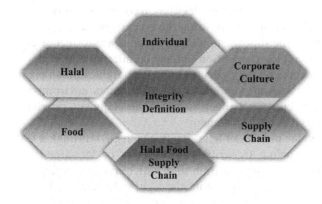

Figure 2.4 Various definition of integrity
Source: Developed by the author, 2019

Halal integrity means that the products remain halal from the upstream to downstream supply chain, free from any activities that might intentionally or unintentionally breach the halal status. There is little research on halal food in Malaysia, including the importance of halal integrity; however, from the researcher's knowledge, there are limited empirical studies from the HLSP perspective. Furthermore, it was recorded that most of the past research was conducted in qualitative methods to establish the concerns and identify the framework regarding the topic. Therefore, it is interesting to investigate the determinant of halal supply chain integrity from the perspective of HLSP in Malaysia.

Additionally, Price WaterHouse Coopers mentioned in their article "From vulnerable to valuable: how integrity can transform a supply chain" that integrity in supply chain must be encompassed in two dimension that is operational and reputed. However, companies must adhere to all aspects of integrity in their supply chain management. Companies recognize that investments to enhance the integrity of supply chains are not only necessary to improve operations, but can also set one apart from the competition (Sussman, 2008). This will steer towards higher operational discipline and enhancement on cost savings. This desirable approach, but dramatic changes in the business environment are absolutely necessary. The ability of the supply chain in meeting objectives such as quality, productivity and financial performance is referred to as operational integrity. The supply chain ability to protect and enhance the brand reputation, customer engagement and investor care, as well as the legislation compliance is referred to as reputational integrity. In addition, the executives are vulnerable towards the risks in the supply chain integrity, such as product safety, business ethics involving corruption, money laundering and bribery, condition of workplace, the intellectual property right, human right and development issue on community, security, green environment (carbon footprint – climate change), economic development, purchasing, impact of product to environment.

As a summary, the process of halal integrity must go through a few processes as stated below: Integrity is ethical belief of doing the right things. Integrity covers organization and individuals. Organization culture is the state of act to promote the right culture to be implemented by the entire organization with starts from strong and positive leadership from top to down. Organization integrity also cover employee's wellbeing and employee selection. The individual personality is the willingness and readiness of individual to uphold trust and belief in individual character. Halal integrity is the act of keeping the whole process in accordance to the halal principal in the supply chain from the upstream and downstream. Integrity in supply chain is referred to as the ability to adhere to the requirements in terms of objective, quality, productivity and financial performance.

Part II
The Constituents and Consequences of Halal Supply Chain Integrity

Case of Malaysia

3 The Overview of HSCI Study in Malaysia

Halal logistics is the main potential business for Malaysia to be the preferred world halal hub, according to the Third *Industrial* Master Plan (IMP3) 2006–2020. The Malaysian Ministry of International Trade and Industry (MITI) statement shows very few LSPs that offer complete halal logistics services. However, halal logistics is gaining public interest and lucrative business. The quality aspects of food safety and traceability are the food consumers' primary concern, especially with increasing demand in the halal food industry (Zulfakar, 2015; Novais et al., 2020). Consumers' concerns from the recent fraudulent occurrence in halal certification and physical contamination on the halal product had reflected and tarnished the halal food industry (Zailani et al., 2010). Therefore, a robust approach to ensuring halal integrity in the supply chain could stabilize the food industry (Tieman et al., 2012). However, a big challenge for all stakeholders in maintaining halal integrity is fully understanding the process throughout the whole supply chain (Zulfakar et al., 2014).

Halal knowledge and awareness are crucial for an employee to handle the overall halal operational process. Priority must be given, especially by all the stakeholders, to ensure that the halal procedure in the supply chain is followed without any compromise (Majid Z.A. et al., 2019). Despite the importance, this stakeholder is not fully aware of and understands the halal supply chain's entire process due to its complexity (Talib et al., 2013). Many studies on the food supply chain have been conducted because there are many food industries issues. The issue of consumer awareness and understanding the halal principles, mixing halal and non- halal products, halal certification and logo compliance with Shariah law and lack of regulation and enforcement need serious attention by all parties along the supply chain. The challenges occur mainly in the halal food segregation and halal traceability of the products (Hijrah et al., 2016). As a matter of fact, traceability

DOI: 10.4324/9781003305682-6

is necessary to track and trace halal critical points in every stage or network of the supply chain (Zailani et al., 2010; Tieman, 2007). At the same time, it is also vital to mention quality control and traceability as the critical components towards determinant of halal supply chain integrity as it is highly sought from the origin to the last point of sale to consumers. With that in mind, halal traceability plays an integral part in increasing halal accountability as a traceability method for the supply chain.

The former researcher agreed that the existing tool needs to be developed for halal traceability, namely the global system monitoring (GSM), radio frequency identification device (RFID) and internet technology. However, the former technology used to validate halal status is manually operated, prone to fraud, lack of security, timely to trace or track, inefficient in real-time monitoring and not accessible to all consumers (Zulfakar et al., 2012). Therefore, challenges in managing the traceability of halal product whereabouts in the supply chain network's complexity.

As for the quality assurance practice in an organization, they are upholding halal integrity could not be guaranteed once it is transported to another destination by other organizations if there is no integration among the halal stakeholder (Jaafar H.S. et al., 2011). Cross-contamination can happen in various stages of the supply chain movement in three areas: warehousing and storage, transportation and terminal interchange (Tieman.M, 2008; Aziz & Zailani, 2016; Karia, 2019). Halal quality assurance is a top priority towards building customer confidence in the halal product brand and a strong company reputation. Halal products' rise in demand is due to the increase in the Muslim population, increasing purchasing power. Muslim buyers are confident with halal-certified products (Aslan & Aslan, 2016). Therefore, it is crucial to ensure halal certification. Halal logo is capable of influencing customer trust and loyalty. However, due to no standardization of halal standards globally, especially in non-Muslim countries, that leads to confusion and misunderstanding and abuse in the halal audit and certification process. The standard variation challenges are unavoidable due to different schools taught in Islam practices and the impossible to develop a 'one-size-fits-all' halal standard in the HSC worldwide.

Zulfakar (2012) mentioned that asset specificity is durable investments, whether physical or human assets, that are exclusively or dedicated to supporting a particular transaction or business partner. Dedicated infrastructures such as transportation fleet, warehouses and storage places, handling equipment to ensure the halal supply chain is free from the element of cross-contamination. It is also equally important that major players in the halal industry show their commitment as they have invested this asset specificity for halal production operations. They have spent enormously to provide dedicated services and facilities to cater to the demand for halal products for customer trust and loyalty. However, most halal LSP did not segregate the product and consolidate halal-certified and non-halal-certified product reasons to achieve economies of scale in their operation cost (Tieman M., 2007).

The halal supply chain partnership's success is throughout the long-term mutual trust and commitment for business sustainability. Tieman (2011) divided HSC into four phases. The first fundamental and crucial element is trust, and second on the halal product phase. The first is between the buyer and seller relationship in dealing with the halal product. Second, the halal product certification or halal marking was in place on the consumer products or seller's outlet.

There is still a lack of academic research in halal logistics and supply chain management (Tieman, 2011). Therefore, this research seeks to contribute knowledge to the theoretical and practical contribution in understanding the determinants of halal supply chain integrity (HSCI) from halal logistics service provider (HLSP) in Malaysia. To the researcher's knowledge, there are limited studies associated with HLSP in the HSC, only a few doctoral theses on halal supply chain (Wan Hassan, 2008; Marzuki, 2012; Tieman, 2013; Zulfakar, 2013; Wan Omar, 2014).

Overall, it can be concluded that there are still issues of inconsistent assessments referring to halal logistics and the practices of halal principles in the halal supply chain (Lai et al., 2020; Mahidin et al., 2019; Mora-Monge et al., 2019). It is also partly contributed by the less state of intervention on halal development among all the stakeholders (M. H. Ali, Tan et al., 2017; M. H. Ali, Zhan et al., 2017; Kottala & Herbert, 2019; Novais et al., 2020). Despite Muslims contributing to the majority of religious practices globally, still, no unified halal standard and logo may be applicable across the globe.

4 The Importance of Halal Integrity in Supply Chain and the Need for Halal Integrity Research

The research focuses on emerging issues in halal supply chain integrity (HSCI) from the halal logistics service providers (HLSP) perspective in Malaysia. Its objective is to enhance halal logistics service provider (HLSP) knowledge, paying high priority to the halal supply chain factors. Halal can be viewed from three perspectives: Religious, business and scholars for research.

First, it is an obligation that should be fulfilled by every Muslim in religious perspectives; second, an excellent business opportunity domestic and internationally, taking advantage of the Muslim population's potential growth and increase of the halal market and third, knowledge nourishment in the research opportunity development from the scholar's perspective.

Understanding the definition of integrity in the complex and dynamic supply chain network is paramount to uphold halal integrity to avoid miscommunication and fraud. This is because the perceptions of halal integrity varied, especially among the halal food supply chain stakeholders, due to differences in scenarios and perspectives. The authenticity and integrity of the halal food supply chain are vital as it becomes the prerequisite in determining the potential business growth for sustainability. Consumers, especially Muslims, are concerned about the integrity of the halal status of the food they consume and the product's origin. There are limited studies on halal integrity from the LSP perspective to the researcher's understanding. This could be a novelty as this paper aims to measure the determinants of halal integrity in Malaysia. Hence, the finding provided a guideline for the policymakers, enforcement authorities, future researchers or halal stakeholders to overview LSP perception on halal integrity.

Recognizing the determinants that uphold halal integrity is the prime consent in ensuring the halalness of the product end to end. Therefore, a common understanding of the determinants of halal

DOI: 10.4324/9781003305682-7

integrity is vital. Halal integrity is becoming a crucial issue to avoid miscommunication and fraud throughout the supply chain process. Having reviewed the literature, the factors of halal integrity was found to be inconsistent from one researcher to another. The notion of halal integrity can be regarded as maintaining the halal status throughout the supply chain network from any activities that might breach the halal status of the product intentionally and unintentionally. The perceptions of halal integrity varied among the halal food supply chain stakeholders due to differences in scenario and perspectives. For instance, this study highlighted five variables on the halal integrity fulfillments: Halal traceability, halal assets specificity, halal quality assurance and trust as the predictors with the measurement of commitments and barriers as control variables.

The authenticity and integrity of the halal supply chain are vital as it becomes the prerequisite in determining the potential business growth for sustainability. Previously, most studies concentrated on halal manufacturers (H. Ahmad et al., 2019; Ustadi et al., 2020). There have been inadequate discussions about halal integrity from the perspective of the industry players despite their paramount roles and responsibility in the halal supply chain. In addition, the study on halal integrity perspective in journals and other publications is limited, which had shown a significantly huge gap in the body of knowledge. The findings of this research will also help the policymakers understand and get a clear picture of the factors that drive halal integrity from the perspective of HLSP in Malaysia. Such knowledge is important as Malaysia has been recognized as a leading country supporting the halal industry worldwide. Malaysia, via the development of Islamic regulatory body, JAKIM (Jabatan Agama Kemajuan Islam, Malaysia) and Halal Development Corporation (HDC) in promoting halal activities are always being referred to and benchmarked by any other countries with regard to the halal matters. Halal is acknowledged as a new horizon of activity in many sectors such as logistics and supply chain, food and restaurant, tourism, banking, textile, medical devices and finance.

To ensure the halal compliance of each sector in the cycle, the Malaysian government needs to get feedback from the industry players of their planned behaviour towards exercising the halal integrity that fulfilled the standards that the halal authorities in Malaysia have regulated. Halal standard, as an example, is a reference book that can guide industry players in establishing their halal business. Although being the main reference for enforcements, the standards were not comprehensive enough in understanding the determinants of achieving halal integrity from the perspective of the HLSP in Malaysia.

Previous research has established the importance of the (Ab Rashid & Bojei, 2019; Haleem & Khan, 2017; Mahidin et al., 2019). A recent study stresses the importance of the halal integrity with creating a critical awareness of the halal needs among the industry players in the food industry (Kwag & Ko, 2019; Mahidin et al., 2019). Halal integrity is a process that not only deals with permitted and prohibited foods, but the halal status of the food product (i.e. from raw materials until it reaches the consumers) should not be breached (i.e. no cross-contamination with the haram product). Earlier studies suggested that halal integrity occurred due to various activities in the supply chain (M. H. Ali, Zhan et al., 2017; Mahidin et al., 2019). However, it has not been clearly defined as what halal integrity can be classified into three elements: individual integrity, corporate integrity and supply chain integrity.

5 HSCI and the Focal of Research

Having this as a background, this research aim to identify the determinant of halal supply chain integrity: The perspective of halal logistics service provider (HLSP) in Malaysia. To have a clear explanation on this issue addressed earlier, the researchers has come out with four research questions as follows:

1 Do halal traceability, halal assets specificity, halal quality assurance, trust, and commitments positively affect halal supply chain integrity?
2 Do halal traceability, halal assets specificity, halal quality assurance and trust have a positive relationship towards commitments?
3 Do commitments mediate the relationship between halal traceability, halal assets specificity, halal quality assurance and trust towards halal supply chain integrity?
4 Do barriers moderate the relationship between commitments towards halal supply chain integrity?

This study is significant to be highlighted since the emerging issues in halal supply chain integrity (HSCI) from the halal logistics service providers (HLSP) perspective in Malaysia. Its objective is to enhance halal logistics service provider (HLSP) knowledge, paying high priority to the halal supply chain factors. In addition, to add value in disseminating information to stakeholders precisely to practitioners and decision-makers of interested parties. Halal can be viewed from three perspectives: Religious, business, and scholars for research. First, it is an obligation that should be fulfilled by every Muslim in religious perspectives; second, an excellent business opportunity domestic and internationally, taking advantage of the Muslim population's potential growth and increase of the Halal market and, third, knowledge

DOI: 10.4324/9781003305682-8

Table 5.1 Summary of Research Questions, Objectives and Hypothesis

Research Questions	Research Objectives	Hypothesis
Does halal traceability, halal assets specificity, halal quality assurance, trust, and commitments positively affect halal supply chain integrity?	To determine whether there is a positive direct relationship between halal traceability, halal assets specificity, halal quality assurance, trust and commitments towards halal supply chain integrity.	Traceability has a significant relationship with halal supply chain integrity. Assets specificity has a significant relationship with halal supply chain integrity. Quality assurance has a significant relationship with halal supply chain integrity. Trust has a significant relationship with halal supply chain integrity. Commitment has a significant relationship with halal supply chain integrity.
Does halal traceability, halal assets specificity, halal quality assurance and trust have a positive relationship towards commitments?	To determine whether there is a positive direct relationship between halal traceability, halal assets specificity, halal quality assurance and trust towards commitments.	Traceability has a significant relationship with commitment. Assets specificity has a significant relationship with commitment. Quality assurance has a significant relationship with commitment. Trust has a significant relationship with commitment.
Does commitments mediate the relationship between halal traceability, halal assets specificity, halal quality assurance and trust towards halal supply chain integrity?	To examine whether commitments mediate the relationship between halal traceability, halal assets specificity, halal quality assurance and trust towards halal supply chain integrity.	Commitment mediates the relationship between traceability and halal supply chain integrity. Commitment mediates the relationship between assets specificity and halal supply chain integrity. Commitment mediates the relationship between quality assurance and halal supply chain integrity. Commitment mediates the relationship between trust and halal supply chain integrity.
Does barriers moderate the relationship between commitments towards halal supply chain integrity?	To examine whether barriers moderate the relationship between commitments towards halal supply chain integrity.	Barriers moderate the relationship between commitment towards halal supply chain integrity.

Source: The authors

nourishment in the research opportunity development from the scholar's perspective.

This research on halal supply chain integrity's determination from halal logistics service provider (HLSP) is crucial for future guidelines. The finding and conclusion will enhance knowledge for HLSP towards economic stability and business sustainability. With the complexity of the halal supply chain, dynamic halal logistics is very vulnerable to business reputation. Therefore, halal supply chain integrity's determination will benefit halal stakeholders, primarily the logistics service provider, in upholding the halal integrity. Table 5.1 shows the detail of the research conduct in relation to HSCI in Malaysia, the research questions, research objectives and research hypotheses.

6 The Five Constituents of Halal Supply Chain Integrity – Halal Traceability, Halal Assets Specificity, Halal Quality Assurance, Halal Trust, Halal Commitments and Halal Barriers

Halal Traceability

Traceability, as defined by The European Commission (2002), is the ability in tracking and tracing the products of food, feed, food-producing animal or substance to be incorporated in the food production, processes and distribution. In addition, Moe (1998), Ab Rashid and Bojei (2019), Poniman et al. (2014) and Zulfakar et al. (2014) mentioned traceability as the ability to track the history and batches as a whole or partial in the production chain from origin through transportation, warehousing, processing, distribution and sales along the supply chain. Additionally, Bakar and Hamid (2013), Ab Rashid and Bojei (2019) and Poniman et al. (2014) stated that traceability is defined as the ability to track food-inclusive ingredients in the network from producers to consumers.

Tracking and tracing is vital to ensure proper product segregation to avoid contamination and damage of the vulnerable product (Zulfikar, 2012). According to Roth et al. (2008), six "T"s in managing product quality in the supply chain included: traceability, transparency, testability, time, trust and training. The attention to this all six "T" is expected to increase the product quality in the supply chain network (Ali et al., 2017). Organizations need to ensure their halal integrity; hence, the practical quality management system concept could provide a systematic and practical approach (JAKIM, 2013). The implementation of HAS is required for multinational companies in order to get Halal certification. This requirement is compulsory for all companies producing halal products in Malaysia. Therefore, the sustainable halal assurance system is a desire to implement systematic traceability by the halal products' manufacturers (Ab Rashid & Bojei, 2019; Abd Rahman et al., 2017; Krishnan et al., 2017; Yusaini H. et al., 2016).

DOI: 10.4324/9781003305682-9

There are inadequate guidelines provided on halal traceability implementation specifically develop for Halal products manufacturers' guidance (Rahman & Abdul, 2018). Any small breach of the Halal assurance system will significantly impact the consumer at the fork end. Consumers are encouraged to look for halal products, which are Toyyib (Riaz & Chaudry, 2004). Consumers need to report any halal product deficiencies to the manufacturer or halal certifiers (Khan et al., 2018).

Halal is a religious obligation (M. H. Ali, Tan et al., 2017), and the demand for halal-certified services and products rises throughout the world (Noorliza, 2020). Halal is concerned with the righteous in handling the slaughter of animals and food preparation (Indarti et al., 2020). The halal products are attractive to non-Muslim consumers for guaranteed in healthier and safe to consume. Therefore, the traceability and halal integrity of products should adhere to halal practices to avoid contamination. Hence, halal logistics training is also deem crucial for a lack of professionalism in the transport and logistics industry (Pahim et al., 2012).

It is the primary concern of all parties to guarantee the halal integrity and avoid risks along the supply chain at all times. Many traceability systems were proposed in the previous studies. Nevertheless, all these systems are centralized, opaque and lack transparency. The logistics innovation, where the blockchain technology is introduced for greater decentralization, visibility and transparency. This supply chain traceability is for the real-time tracing which embedded Islamic dietary law into HACCP, blockchain and the Internet of Things (Rejeb, 2018). The transparency of the actual level of product halalness could be improved from the information flow along the supply chain (Ab Talib et al., 2016; Zailani et al., 2017). Information technology is a critical attribute in technology's advantages and control, significantly impacting logistics and supply chain management (Murphy & Wood, 2004). Besides that, information technology is equally important to link logistics activities in the integration process (Bowersox et al., 2010). Hammant (1995) claimed a need for improvement in supply chain performance to become efficient and open for greater collaboration.

Halal Asset Specificity

Assets specificity is vital to upholding halal integrity through complete segregation along the supply chain (Abdul Rahman et al., 2018). The importance of asset specificity may vary in transportation, warehousing or equipment and could be the critical success factors in halal supply chain integrity (Hanifah et al., 2017; Ngah et al., 2019; Nor et al., 2016). Transportation enables the delivery of a halal product from one place to destination. The logistics process facilitates the various parties to allowed local halal products to be transported and marketed worldwide (Gubbins, 2003). According to Coyle et al. (2011), transportation activities are "the act of moving goods or people from an origin to a required destination. It also includes the creation of time and place utilities". Tseng et al., (2005) mentioned transportation integration in logistics and supply chain management. Transport is the most important economic activity among the components of business logistics (Arif et al., 2019; Mohamed et al., 2018; Soraji et al., 2017). An efficient transportation system will result in logistics efficiency, decrease operating costs, and upgrade service quality. In addition to focusing on delivering goods from one destination to another, transport strategy could attract foreign direct investment (FDI) as a study by Saidi and Hammami (2011).

In the halal supply chain, the assets specificity was highly recommended by several authors and had suggested for complete segregation to separate halal and non-halal products (Riaz & Chaudry, 2004; Soong, 2007; Jaafar et al., 2011; Omar & Jaafar, 2011; Tieman et al., 2012, 2013). The mixing of halal and non-halal in transportation will void the halal status as the non-halal will prevail (Tieman, 2011). Therefore, Tieman (2013) has emphasized that, while it implies a high cost to the logistics provider, the halal logistics service provider handles transport vehicles or containers. Lancioni (2000), on the same note, stated that the logistics added 25–50% of the overall logistical costs, while a method of segregation has been highly realistic (Iberahim et al., 2012; Jaafar et al., 2011; Daud et al., 2011) as shown in the previous investigation.

Halal Quality Assurance

Halal certification is concerned with the quality, safety and hygienic aspects of the food supply chain. The comprehension of halal principles and practices is about the realization of the halal concept that is related to a green environment (Hassan et al., 2015; Tan et al., 2017). Green management is concerned with reducing the negative impact of human activities. Halal food, although it is healthy and safe to be consumed, is more conscious of the quality of the halal product (Yunos et al., 2014). This halal quality standard was applied to the finished and semi-finished products consisting of cosmetics, pharmaceutical, medical products, processed food and comprehensive logistics services (Noordin et al., 2014).

The integration and streamlining of the best practices of halal assurance critical control point (HACCP) is the fundamental of the halal food supply chain. This HACCP is a systematic way to: analyse potential hazards in the food supply chain; identify the critical control points in the food supply chain and decided the critical point of food safety (Pun et al., 2008) and establish a robust halal food supply chain that strives for lower vulnerability to halal contamination (Vlajic et al., 2012).

Key factors affecting HACCP practices covered regulations of food, industry roles in government policies and intervention, training on food safety and hygiene and food contamination, or poisoning. Considered as a new discipline in supply chain management, halal is extended towards logistics, which demonstrated that information, abilities, and staff responsibility are the foundation for HACCP (Fotopoulos et al., 2011). The significant factors affecting the halal assurance critical control point (HACCP) are the regulations in halal foods; the role of industry, policies and interventions of government; food safety and hygiene training; food contamination and poisoning. Therefore, the logistics business process highly required the implementation of the halal management system for halal control and assurance activities (Tieman, 2012). Category of the halal certification user is the manufacturer/producer, sub-contract manufacturer, abattoir/slaughterhouse, distributor/trader, food premise and logistics service providers.

The limitation and challenge of halal certification is that there is no single standard recognized worldwide, and there are numerous certification bodies (Haroon Latif, 2016; Mohd Imran Khan & Abid Haleem, 2016; Muhammad et al., 2018). Lack of proper products/services classification of halal. Halal certification is voluntary and is not compulsory (Ghadikolaei, 2016). The halal certification confirms that halal certified the ingredients used in a product, and the premise is free from haram or non-halal products. It prevents consumer fraud in the preparation, distribution, and sale of halal products and services. JAKIM issues the halal certification, a prerequisite for JAKIM to determine clients' expectations and perceptions in-service evaluation for improvement in halal quality assurance. Zainuddin (2001) mentioned that understanding citizen customers' perceptions and expectations could be achieved through public organizations and the government's reputation.

Recommended implementing an appropriate training program by JAKIM for their personnel at all levels to meet their customer's expectations. Emphasis on human factors in service delivery, customer care, work ethics, and human relations skill. Training in customer relationships is essential, and this applies to employees of all levels. Apart from that, JAKIM could train their staff to cater to clients' needs and provide them with a good experience when dealing with the certification body to ensure the Halal products' credibility and integrity (Badruldin et al., 2012).

The government has made an effort towards establishing research and innovation through collaboration with the higher learning institutions to promote halal knowledge. These integrative activities are crucial for the enhancement of halal supply chain performance. The local universities involved are namely Universiti Putra Malaysia, UPM (Halal Product Research Institute, HPRI), International Islamic University Malaysia, IIUM (International Institute for Halal Research and Training, INHART), Universiti Teknologi MARA, UiTM (Malaysia Institute of Transport Research, MITRANS) and more. Their focus is on halal training, research, certification assistance, offering entrepreneurship opportunities, and signifying towards the government objectives (Yasin, 2011).

JAKIM had certified 32 training providers to conduct halal certification training based on the Malaysian Halal Management System. One of Malaysia Halal Certification requirements is: "Halal executive is compulsory to have a Halal Executive Certificated from JAKIM Certified Training Providers." In the future, it will be compulsory for a company to have a dedicated Halal executive for them to comply with the new Malaysia Halal Standard.

Halal Trust

Through the reviewed literature, three critical perspectives of trust are found in the supply chain relationship (Indarti et al., 2020). First, the characteristics of trust; second, rational trust, which included cost and benefit, dynamic capabilities and technology and, third, the institutional trust or security system. There are challenges in measuring and calculating the perceptions of trust in terms of uncertainty and risk to translate into the trust factor.

According to Mayer et al. (1995), one does not need to risk anything in trust; however, it must take the risk for the engagement of action in trusting (Selim et al., 2019). The mechanism of coping risk levels and bearable limits of trust can be risk management or security management. Hence, trust and risk can be equated as risk is equal to no trust; no risk is equal to trust; risk worthy is equal to trustworthy (Al-Ansi et al., 2019). The prospect of confidence leads to reliability, integrity, perception, reliability, sincerity, goodwill, compassion, dedication, justice, emotions, etc.

Mayer et al. (1995) mentioned that trust is constructed from the partner's level of willingness to take the risk of perceived benevolence and integrity. Additionally, trust is constructed based on commonality and personal experience (Tan & Thoen, 2001); similarly, based on the history of reliability and discrete behaviour, integrity and honesty, benevolence, caring and altruism (Sheppard & Sherman, 1998). Laeequddin et al. mentioned the need to measure trust from a different perspective and identify among the supply chain members in future research. The subject of trust is viewed as a complicated and multifaceted concept despite the availability of abundant literature. Trust measurement approached should be from multilevel risk perspectives.

The industry of halal food in the last few years has grown substantively worldwide. Increasingly crucial for Muslim consumers to pursue safety, hygiene and quality assurance. In-addition to adhering to the Shariah, food that they consume should be Halalan-thoyyiban, lawful, authentic, safe and wholesome (Zailani et al., 2017). The halal food manufacturers in Malaysia should comply with MS1500:2009 on the halal certification (halal Logo). However, the improper preparation and improper description of halal food have significant impacts on the demand for halal food, and buyers trust to consume halal food (Noorliza, 2020). Hence, trust is a crucial element in upholding halal integrity by all parties in the supply chain. HACCP practices are affected by the following factors such as food regulation, the role of industry, government policies and interventions, training on food safety, hygiene contamination and poisoning (Pun & Bhairo-Beekhoo, 2008).

Trust in brand, according to MF Shamsudin et al. (2020), Huang (2017), Kotler (2017), is the most valuable asset for a business as customers put high reliability and believed in the service offered. This could prosper through communication and information to customers. The business organization's product or service's characteristics and benefits should be made known to their customers.

Halal Commitment

Staff commitment, knowledge and skill are crucial to HACCP implementation (Fotopoulos et al., 2011). Similarly, the food safety management system as the food processor's quality needs to be controlled and assured (M. H. Ali & Suleiman, 2018). Additionally, the logistics business processes are needed to emphasize halal control and assurance activities (Tieman, 2012). According to Alfalla-Luque et al. (2015), commitment and internal integration of employees, before external, reinforced by management at a strategic level, are rather crucial for the supply chain's success and mitigation of barriers.

According to Ik-Whan and Taewon (2005), the increase in trust will determine the increase in willingness to commit for specific matters, vice-versa as trust and commitment are interrelated. Parties in the supply chain must uphold a certain level of commitment to strengthen and establish trust between all parties (Mahidin et al., 2019; Mora-Monge et al., 2019; Tarmizi et al., 2014). The visibility of trust and commitment in the supply chain partners will be visible when both organizations are willing to increase their investment in asset specificity to serve their partners' unique needs (Lu et al., 2006).

According to (Ahmed, 2019), the buyers' ability to apply halal certification for raw materials and ingredients and enrol employees in halal food handling education is essential to the awareness of halal food supply chain integrity. All parties in the halal food supply chain should share responsibility in protecting and uphold halal integrity to the highest level by displaying a high level of commitment (Zulfakar et al., 2014).

However, commitment is implied as work responsibilities, obligations, dedication and persistence, honouring their agreement, and persistence in keeping their promises (M. H. Ali, Zhan et al., 2017; Lai et al., 2020). Additionally, commitment is considered an attitude of perseverance; to fulfil one's duties, complete their task, responsibilities and promises to adhere to their values and beliefs. Second, they displayed an attitude of never give up until they reached their goal accomplishment. Mason (2001) declared commitment as the ethics of integrity.

Halal Barriers

Past research highlighted that among the challenge of halal integrity is the lack of enforcement and compliances (Aziz & Zailani, 2016; Susanty et al., 2020). Service providers in the Halal supply chain as well as halal logistics experiences unresolvod issues related to compliances standards (Mohamed et al., 2020). Such a situation lead to a grey area of integrity implementation by the service providers in the industry. Recent research claimed that the rules provided by the authorities are rigid but lack of enforcement caused many service providers to tend to operate without following the standards procedures (Selim et al., 2019). However, the process of applications to be certified keeps the potential service providers from the halal industry (Zailani et al., 2017).

It was highlighted that the process of certifications was not clear. A qualitative study conducted in Malaysia on third party logistic providers revealed that the terms and implementation between halal organisations were different (Ngah et al., 2015). Such a situation creates confusion among the halal industry players and hindered new players from a venture into the halal industry (Bashir et al., 2019). Apart from that, the compliance-related matters were reported to be the barriers between the service providers commitment towards integrity (Ab Talib et al., 2016).

It was also stated that the long-waited halal certification process led to some unethical issues by service providers (Zulfakar et al., 2014). The process of certifications took six months to a year due to unfriendly steps and tests that need to be done. It can be concluded that only selected logistic service providers are interested in following the process. Such situations were seen as a barrier for the halal industry related to supply chain and logistics to expand (Ahmad & Shariff, 2016). Many large logistic providers with strong businesses may not be focused at the halal industry due to the process (Abdul Rahman et al., 2018).

According to (Tieman, 2011) the government needs to be meticulous and accurate in analysing the details to ensure the product is halal and the process was followed. It was also reported that other barriers factors among the service providers are finances and lack of manpower (Susanty et al., 2020). On top of that service providers need to invest in their asset to fulfil the Halal requirements (Selim et al., 2019).

Past study highlighted a need for government to make the process clear in halal compliance with shariah requirements to ensure its integrity (Maulan et al., 2016; Poniman et al., 2014; Zakaria & Abdullah, 2019). According to (Butt et al., 2017) consumers will lose their confidence in the halal status should there is lack of integrity. Integrity issues will lead to poor in sales and business will be affected. Therefore, it is important to ensure that the halal standards have the highest integrity guarantee (Ahmad & Shariff, 2016).

Past studies also highlighted the role of government agencies in supporting the halal integrity especially related to halal supply chain. Government agencies is expected to provide more professional training and courses to equip service providers with awareness about halal compliance (Nor et al., 2016). On the other part, it was also highlighted the need for support in consultation and customer support towards halal integrity and compliance (Ab Talib et al., 2016). Recent research underlines the need for top management of service providers to have commitments towards the halal supply chain integrity (Ngah et al., 2014). It was reported that trust and commitments are among the important issues that need to be managed within the organizations. Lack of awareness and trust resulted to additional barriers towards the integrations (Tieman, 2011). Commitment among the service providers is important as they play a vital role in the operationalization and execution of the halal integration (Poniman et al., 2014).

In conclusion, halal supply chain integration's barrier resulted in many concerns areas among the service providers. Many of the services providers claimed that commitment alone was not enough to support the relationship towards halal integration (Garepasha et al., 2020; Haleem et al., 2020; Selim et al., 2019; Shamsudin et al., 2020). Thus this study is measuring the role of barriers towards halal integrations. Figures 6.1 and 6.2 below illustrate the theoretical framework develop from this study the develop hypotheses on HSCI. While Table 6.1 lists the details of each hypotheses examined in the study.

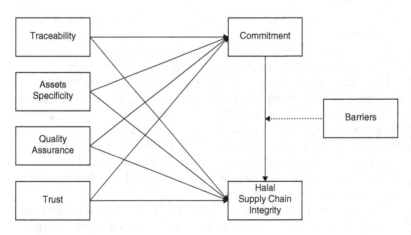

Figure 6.1 Theoretical framework
Source: The authors

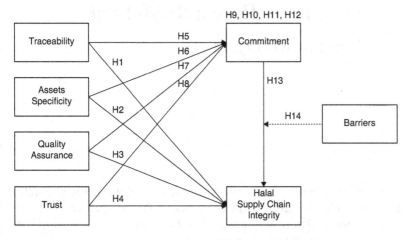

Figure 6.2 Hypotheses development in HSCI case study in Malaysia
Source: The authors

Table 6.1 List of Hypotheses Developed in HSCI Case Study in Malaysia

H#	Statements
H1	Traceability has a significant relationship with halal supply chain integrity.
H2	Assets specificity has a significant relationship with halal supply chain integrity.
H3	Quality assurance has a significant relationship with halal supply chain integrity.
H4	Trust has a significant relationship with halal supply chain integrity.
H5	Traceability has a significant relationship with commitment.
H6	Assets specificity has a significant relationship with commitment.
H7	Quality assurance has a significant relationship with commitment.
H8	Trust has a significant relationship with commitment.
H9	Commitment mediates the relationship between traceability and halal supply chain integrity.
H10	Commitment mediates the relationship between assets specificity and halal supply chain integrity.
H11	Commitment mediates the relationship between quality assurance and halal supply chain integrity.
H12	Commitment mediates the relationship between trust and halal supply chain integrity.
H13	Commitment has a positive relationship with halal supply chain integrity.
H14	Barriers moderate the relationship between commitment towards halal supply chain integrity.

Source: The authors

7 HSCI and Research Method
Case of Malaysia

This study applied a quantitative research method. In survey research, the data collection instrument describes its features, characteristics, and contents (Sekaran & Bougie, 2016). The next section described the survey questionnaire for this study.

Development of Questionnaires

The purpose of this empirical quantitative study is on determinants of halal supply chain integrity from the halal logistics service provider perspective on halal traceability, halal assets specificity, halal quality assurance and, trust and commitment. The questionnaire was developed in relation to research questions covering information, decisions, and actions to collect data from target participants. This study also intended to measure the relationship between those constructs. Thus, a survey questionnaire is the most appropriate instrument to access the variable of interest from the targeted respondent. It is the most common data collection instrument (Sekaran & Bougie, 2016). In the questionnaire development, the desired analysis plan and type of scale need to be identified accordingly. The questionnaire was derived from selected previous exploratory studies and redesigned to serve this quantitative analysis. Formal preparation and supervision were carried out in order to assess the scale and the components. The expert opinion of academics and industry was drawn up to ensure that the questions were correctly formulated to serve this research's objectives. Good questionnaire creation may attract citation in the future should there is any replication of future research. Dr. Intan Salwani Mohamed of UiTM assisted the creation of questionnaires during her "workshop on the design of questionnaires."

According to Rowley (2014), it is essential to ensure the information relevancy, specific data needs and rationale for each item in developing

DOI: 10.4324/9781003305682-10

the questionnaire design. Since this research is quantitative-based, questionnaires are developed that consists of seven sections.

Section 1 consists of demographic information. Demographic questions are related to the company profile, halal logistics service provider, company address, contact person, position in the organization, religion, age group, number of years of working experience, HLSP number of employees, number of years in the HLSP company. Overall, these 12 demographic questions have sufficiently captured the demographic profile of the samples.

Section 2 consists of measurement from the halal logistics service provider perspective, based on halal traceability, aalal assets specificity, halal quality assurance, trust, commitment and halal supply chain integrity. The dimension for halal traceability is five items on Information & Communication Technology (ICT), three items on logistics control and two items on innovative capability. The dimension for halal assets specificity is four on resource availability, three items on physical segregation and three on investment. The dimension for halal quality assurance is three items on Halal Policy, three items on Halal Standard and four on Halal certification. The dimension for trust is three items on customer relationship, two items on Halal risk management and four items on company policy. The dimension for commitment is five items on management responsibility, five items on Halal training and five items on halal personnel. The dimension for halal supply chain integrity is two items on the HSC management system and two items on maintenance of HSC and two items on the role of government.

Details of the questionnaire are as per Appendix 1. It is further explained in the variable section on the following topic.

The response patterns are based on an interval scaled (Likert). The scale is arranged by 1–5, representing the agreement's level with the survey questionnaire's statement (Synodinos, 2003). Scale one represents strongly disagree, and five represent strongly agree. The Likert scale is reliable and has been widely used in past research. Likert scale is relatively simple, and the nature of results is based on a numerical scale (Hibberd & Bennett, 1990). There have been arguments on the appropriate number of points to be used on the Likert-type scale. The length of the scales needs to be determined by the study's nature and the respondents' ability to differentiate among the levels (Lewin, 2005). While according to Cohen et al. (2000), the application of a five point scale rating promotes more responsive and sensitive fieldwork.

Apart from coding the statements for ease of data capture for analysis, they were worded in a simple, clear, concise, and short manner to enable easy comprehension by the respondents to minimize the risk of high blank responses (Rowley, 2014). In summary, the questionnaire was designed to maximize the respondent's motivation to answer the question. Simultaneously, to minimize the difficulty, they could provide an accurate response and effectively contribute to the research outcome.

Items Used for Questionnaires

All items were extracted from a collection of previous studies before professional modification to meet the study's research questions and objectives. Tables 7.1–7.8 below is a summary of the items used for the research. This research consists of 60 self-rating items on a five-point Likert scale format, ranging from '1' "strongly disagree" to '5' "strongly agree."

Table 7.1 Summary of Variables and Items Used in this Study

Variables	Source	Dimensions	Items
Halal supply chain integrity	Z.A. Majid (2019)	HSC management system, maintenance of halal supply chain, role of government	6
Traceability	Z.A. Majid (2019)	ICT, logistics control, innovative capability	10
Asset specificity	Z.A.Majid (2019)	Resource, physical segregation, investment	10
Quality assurance	(Ab Rashid & Bojei, 2019; Ambali & Bakar, 2013, 2014)food companies must be prepared to implement systematic traceability system to ensure the authenticity of Halal products and comprehend the importance of Halal industry environmental factors (HIEF	Halal policy, halal standard, halal certification	10

Variables	Source	Dimensions	Items
Trust	(A. Ali et al., 2018a, 2018b; Quoquab et al., 2019; Vanany, Soon, et al., 2019)there is a dearth of study that has examined the impact of halal logo toward customer loyalty. To fulfill this gap, this study aims to shed some light on the impact of halal logo toward achieving customer loyalty in the context of fast food industry in Malaysia. More specifically, the objectives of this study are: to examine the direct and indirect effect of halal logo on customer loyalty; to examine the effect of halal logo on trust and perceived reputation; to examine the effect of halal logo and perceived reputation on customer loyalty; and to examine the mediating effect of trust and perceived reputation in the relationship between halal logo and customer loyalty among the fast food industry consumers in Malaysia. Design/methodology/approach: This study used stimulus-organism-response (S-O-R	Customer relationship, halal risk management, company policy	9
Commitment	(Tieman & Ghazali, 2014; Wan Ismail et al., 2020)warehousing and terminals as a proof of a halal logistics system. Next to an extensive literature review, focus group sessions have been conducted in Malaysia, the Netherlands and China in identifying halal control activities and assurance activities in logistics business processes. The findings show that product characteristics (bulk versus unitized, ambient versus a cool chain	Management responsibility, halal training, halal personnel	15

(Continued)

Variables	Source	Dimensions	Items
Barriers	(Farooque et al., 2019; Haleem et al., 2019)this paper develops a theoretical framework for identifying relevant barriers to integrating circular economy philosophy in food supply chain management. The study uses 105 responses from Chinese food supply chain stakeholders including food processors, sales and distribution channels, consumers and government officials. It applies a fuzzy decision-making trial and evaluation laboratory (DEMATEL	Enforcements, standards, supports	16

Source: Z.A. Majid (2019)

Table 7.2 Likert Scales

Strongly Disagree	Disagree	Neutral	Agree	Strongly Agree
1	2	3	4	5

Table 7.3 Halal Supply Chain Measurement

Items for Halal Supply Chain Integrity
1 Our organization believe that Halal Traceability is the determinant of HSC integrity for HLSP
2 Our organization believe Trust is the determinant of HSC integrity for HLSP

Maintenance of Halal Supply Chain
3 Our organization believe Halal Quality Assurance is the determinant of HSC integrity for HLSP
4 Our organization believe that Assets Specificity is the determinant of HSC integrity for HLSP

Role of Government
5 Our organization believe that role of government is crucial in exploring the innovative idea in the HSC
6 Our organization believe the government-industry relationship will encourage strong bonding toward profitability

Source: Z.A. Majid (2019)

Table 7.4 Traceability Measurement

Items for Traceability

Information & Communication Technology (ICT)
1 Our organization believe that ICT is important for Halal Traceability
2 Our organization use ICT to monitor real-time tracking
3 Our organization believe the usage of ICT will expedite the customs clearance process forHLSP
4 Our organization feel satisfied with the current Halal Traceability Systems
5 Our organization need to upgrade the current Halal Traceability systems for improvement

Logistics Control
6 Our organization believe an effective Halal Traceability System will improve service quality to customers
7 Our organization monitor shipment reach within schedule through a traceability system
8 Our organization have good logistics control on shipment movement

Innovative Capability
9 Our organization do inspire employees toward innovative ideas on Halal traceability
10 Our organization do encourage employees toward innovative ideas to improve Halal traceability

---

Source: Z.A. Majid (2019)

Table 7.5 Asset Specificity Measurement

Items for asset specificity

Resource
1 Our organization provide infrastructure for warehousing facilities in ensuring HSC integrity
2 Our organization provide infrastructure for transport facilities in ensuring HSC integrity
3 Our organization provide assets specificity as recommended by the Halal authority
4 Our organization have the resource available to cater to our customer's need

Physical segregation
5 Our organization ensure the appropriate transport for a different type of customers halal products
6 Our organization provides a dedicated warehouse for the storage of our customers' halal products
7 Our organization ensure a dedicated vehicle to transport our customers' halal products

(Continued)

Investment
8   Our organization believe in the need for financial stability for assets specificity investment
9   Our organization believe that investment in the asset specificity will be a return on investment (ROI)
10 Our organization is willing to invest in asset specificity to cater to our customer's need

Source: Z.A. Majid (2019)

Table 7.6 Quality Assurance Measurement

Items for quality assurance

Halal policy
1   Our organization shared our halal policy with all employees to ensure quality assurance
2   Our organization follow halal policy for the quality assurance improvement
3   Our organization have a competent internal halal committee to advise on halal policy

Halal standard
4   Our organization have a written halal standard as a guideline to all employees
5   Our organization are aware of the halal standard ms2400 halal supply chain
6   Our organization follow the halal standard & practices for quality assurance in ensuring HSC integrity

Halal certification
7   Our organization understand the process of halal certification
8   Our organization has halal executive to handle our halal matters inquiries
9   Our organization has trained employees to manage our customers' halal shipment
10 Our organization follow the guideline of halal certification for audit purposes

Source: Z.A. Majid (2019)

Table 7.7 Trust Measurement

Items for trust

Customers relationship
1 Our organization build trust in customers relationship for business sustainability
2 Our organization believe in the importance of Trust in building customers relationship
3 Our organization have a customer's loyalty program for long term business collaboration

Halal risk management
4 Our organization believes that halal risk management is important for HLSP
5 Our organization follow the guideline in the halal risk management

Company policy
6 Our organization written company policy is a guideline for all employees
7 Our organization believe that all employees must understand the company policy
8 Our organization's company policy is trustworthy to all stakeholders
9 Our organization have introductory of company policy to all new employees

---

Source: Z.A. Majid (2019); A. Ali et al. (2018a, 2018b; Quoquab et al. (2019); Vanany, Soon, et al. (2019)

Table 7.8 Commitments Measurement

Management responsibility

Items for commitments
1 Our organization are committed to our customers' requirement
2 Our organization believe in the importance of commitment in customers relationship
3 Our organization believe that all employees are committed to our customers' requirement
4 Our organization have developed a customer's loyalty program
5 Our organization always give quality service for customers retention

Halal training
6 Our organization are committed to halal training for all employee
7 Our organization engage with local halal authority for training to our employee
8 Our organization always trained our employees for customers satisfaction
9 Our organization have a halal training program to ensure halal Supply chain awareness
10 Our organization are reliable at all time in ensuring HSC integrity

(Continued)

Halal personnel
11 Our organization have a dedicated internal halal committee
12 Our organization emphasis qualified halal personnel to handle customers halal shipment
13 Our organization encourage transparency in managing customers complain
14 Our organization selected halal Personnel who are qualified in halal supply chain experience
15 Our organization emphasize that halal personnel uphold halal integrity in handling customers halal shipment

Source: Z.A. Majid (2019)

Measurement

In this research, the measure proposed in this study is adopted and modified as per details in Table 7.9. All items are measured using a five-point Likert scale. Respondents are asked relevant questions based on the list of items in the following table. The items used are shown in the table below.

Table 7.9 Barriers Measurement

Items for barriers

1 Weak enforcement on compliances
2 Unresolved issues for standards and practices
3 lack of clarity in halal definition by different halal organizations
4 Lack of innovation, research and development (R&D) on compliance-related work
5 Lack of professional program/training program/
6 Lack of support from the government and regulatory bodies
7 weak enforcement of rules/norms
8 Inadequate (unified) customer support from halal certifying organizations
9 Complicated systems and processes
10 Lack of technology and related issues and their weak compliances
11 Lack of facilities of infrastructure
12 Lack of professional and universally accepted halal certifying organization
13 Lack of consumer awareness, support, attitude and image development
14 Higher cost of halal implementation
15 Lack of top management support and change management
16 Insufficient planning regarding halal implementation

Source: (Farooque et al., 2019; Haleem et al., 2019).

All variables mentioned in Tables 7.1–7.8 used in this analysis were measured using multiple items from previous studies, except for demographic factors. The phrasing of the objects, however, was altered to suit the sample and local setting.

Population and Sample

The total halal logistics service provider (HLSP) certified by JAKIM in 2018 is 86 and in 2019 increased to 130 companies. In 2017, there were a total of 6000 JAKIM-certified halal companies in Malaysia. In 2018, there was an increase from 20% to 7204. This increase in result indicates that Malaysia has a strong influence on the global halal position in 2020. The halal industry's growth had contributed to great opportunities for domestic and international logistics service providers in Malaysia. As halal products are being accepted worldwide, Malaysia plays a crucial role as the major exporter among the Organization of Islamic Cooperation (OIC) countries. Past research on halal logistics indicated a similarly small amount of sampling due to a limited population as per Table 7.10

Population

The population refers to the entire group of people, events, or things of interest that the researcher wishes to investigate (Sekaran & Bougie, 2016). This study's total population is the overall number of the halal

Table 7.10 Population Sampling

No	Author/Year	Topic	Sampling
1	(Noorliza, 2020)	Halal resource capability	123 third party logistics
2	(Susanty et al., 2020)	The barrier of Halal logistics	23 companies related to F&B
3	(Ab Rashid & Bojei, 2019)	Halal supply chain	127 respondents from SME managers that participated in MIHAS
4	(Karia, 2019)	Halal practices in logistics and warehouse	129 respondents from the Malaysian logistics directory
5	(Zailani et al., 2018)	Halal logistics	253 F&B firms in Malaysia

logistics service provider (HLSP) as an actor in the halal supply chain. The mutual collaboration and linkages between the government and industry are crucial to encourage the growth of HLSP. Till to date, the total number of HLSP certified by JAKIM in 2019 is 130 but it was 86 in 2018, an increase of about 50%. The researcher's coverage is 100% of the total population sampling.

This research's scope will generally focus on the critical five research objectives and questions. The independent variable was adopted and adapted from the exploratory study by Hafiz Zulfakar (2012), Ab Talib (2020), Noorliza (2020), Raut et al. (2019) and Tieman and Ghazali (2014) on factors that influence the Halal supply chain integrity. The halal industry is lucrative and supported by the halal management system and demanded halal LSPs to emphasize their upholding halal integrity. According to Chua (2012), sampling is selecting several subjects from a population. At the same time, Sekaran and Bougie (2016) added that the sample is a subset of the population.

Sample Size and Sampling Procedure

Determining the optimal sample size for a study assures adequate power to detect statistical significance (Chua, 2012). Sampling is the process of selecting a sufficient number of the right elements from the population (Sekaran & Bougie, 2016). In this study, 130 HLSP will be involved in data distribution and collection. This study will make use of the total target population for data collection. The total target population, sampling table Krejcie and Morgan (1970), is referred (as per Appendix B) to determine the sampling size for each HLSP. The calculation was based on $p = 0.05$, where the probability of committing a Type I error is less than 5%, or $p < .05$ (Chua, 2012).

In determining the sample size for research, various factors were considered, such as timing, budget, and degree of confidence level (Hair et al., 2003). Therefore, some guidelines must be followed to determine the appropriate sample size. According to Roscoe (1975), the appropriate number of samples is between 30 and 500. However, Comrey and Lee (1992) suggested that the best sample size is between 300 and 1000. According to Meyers et al. (2013), the sample size should not be smaller than 200 respondents for a single study.

In this study, based on Krejcie and Morgan (1970) table, the targeted sample size is 97. In contrast, Hair et al. (2013) suggested calculating sample size based on ten times the number of variables in the most complex construct. In contrast, Hair et al. (2013) suggested calculating sample size based on ten times the number of variables in the most complex construct. In this study, the most complex construct is a commitment, which consists of 15 measurement items. Thus, the minimum sample based on the ten times rule is 150 (10 × 15=150). Based on the references mentioned above and suggestions, this study's sample size is described in Table 7.11, The total samples are 217, which is met the minimum suggested number of samples by all references.

First, to determine the sample size for each selected HLSP, proportionate stratified sampling was deployed. This method also was deployed in earlier researches by Rahim (2018), Dawi (2016) and Edward (2013). Based on Sekaran and Bougie (2016), the calculation of proportionate stratified sampling depends on the sub-population number.

In this study, data were collected by a survey method using self-administered questionnaires. According to Sekaran and Bougie (2016),

Table 7.11 Background of EOA Panels

Panel	Name	Position	Field/Expertise
A	Dato Ts Abd Radzak Malek FCILT	International President The Chartered Institute of Logistics & Transport (CILT)	Transport, logistics & supply chain
B	Prof. Dr. Faridah Hj Hassan	Prof. InQKA Institute of Quality & Knowledge Advancement, UiTM Shah Alam, Selangor	Professor of halal, marketing & strategic management
C	Dr. Muhammad Nizam Bin Baharom FCILT	Presiden Persatuan Pengusaha Logistik Bumiputra Selangor	Transport, logistics & supply chain
D	Dr. Mohd Iskandar Bin Illyas Tan	Deputy Director UTM-Halal Technology Consortium (UTM-HTC) Principal Research at Halal Informatics (HOLISTIC)	Technology/ research halal supply chain
E	Associate Professor Ts. Dr. Zuraimi Bin Abdul Aziz	Director UMK Centre For External Education (UMKCEE)	Transport, logistics & supply chain management
F	Dr. Harlina Suzana Jaafar	Director Malaysia Institute of Transport (MITRANS) Chairman (SMIIC) MS2400 Halal Supply Chain	Halal supply chain research & management

Source: The authors

this type of survey instrument is appropriate since a self-administered questionnaire is inexpensive; however, it can produce a high response rate, straightforward, and easy to understand. The use of the Likert scale eases respondents to manage and choose the correct answer. The questionnaire distribution process was administered closely by the researcher for each of the selected HLSP. This is to ensure a high return rate, and the right samples were selected for each HLSP.

Expert Validation

The purpose of conducting expert validation is to allow judgement on the content of the survey instrument. According to Karim et al. (2008), content validity is a judgement, by an expert, of the extent to which a question truly measures the concept it is intended to measure. In this study, Expert Opinion Assessment (EOA) helped the researcher understand the research area, measurement items, and appropriateness for data collection and analysis.

Appointment letters to EOA panels are shown in appendix C and C-1, respectively. In addition, opinions and comments from the EOA process supported the researcher in developing more qualified data collection instruments. In this research, six experts in the related field of this study have reviewed a set of the questionnaire. The recommendation and suggestions by the EOA panels are considered. The summary of EOA panels is as per Table 7.11. Feedback and comments were gathered based on the exercises, followed by corrections according to comments and concerns. Overall, the comments mainly related to the used of terms, vocabulary, sentences and grammar. All points highlighted took into considerations before the final data collection was done.

Pilot Study

A pilot test was conducted to decide the actual instrument to be utilized in this study. According to Cooper and Schindler (2011), the targeted pilot's size might range from 25 to 100 subjects. Chua (2012) mentioned that the number is generally from 20–40 people with a similar demographic background. In addition, the respondents do not have to be statistically selected. A pilot study was performed to correct any instrument's inadequacies before data collection and identify wording and translation difficulties. The reliability test for each instrument was calculated using the pilot study data (Sekaran & Bougie, 2016). The pilot study provided an idea regarding the sampling plan's response rate and adequateness to improve the research (Neuman,

2007). Cronbach's alpha reliability coefficients for the scales' internal consistency as one of the criteria for selecting past instruments. Cronbach's coefficient alpha was used as the common method for assessing the reliability of a measurement scale with multi-point items (Pallant, 2001). Coefficient alpha can range from 0.0 (no reliability) to 1.0 (perfect reliability).

However, good reliability should produce at least a coefficient value of 0.7 (Hair et al., 1995; Pallant, 2001). For exploratory research, the Cronbach's α values greater than 0.7 can be considered high reliability; less than 0.6 is considered poor. Only those with Cronbach's α values less than 0.5 should be discarded (Sekaran & Bougie, 2016). From another perspective, Chua (2013) stated that the Cronbach's Alpha value of 0.65 to 0.95 is satisfactory, while the value of less than 0.65 is low reliability.

Thus, items that have an alpha value of less than 0.65 must be dropped. However, a value that exceeds 0.95 is considered too high and could cause overlapping items. Tables 7.12 and 7.13 further explains Cronbach's Alpha value.

Table 7.12 Cronbach's Alpha Value

Alpha Value	Clarification
<0.6	Poor
0.6–0.7	Moderate
0.7–0.8	Good
0.8–0.9	Excellent
>0.9	Strongly Good

Source: Sekaran & Bougie, 2016

Table 7.13 Fornell Larker's Criterion

	Assets Specificity	Barriers	Commitment	Halal Supply Chain	Quality Assurance	Traceability	Trust
AS1	0.853						
AS2	0.849						
AS3	0.882						
AS4	0.727						
AS5	0.794						
AS6	0.828						
AS7	0.810						
BAR1		0.915					
BAR10		0.938					

In this study, a pilot test was conducted with five HLSP. Convenient sampling has been used in selecting the respondents for the pilot study. The purpose of the pilot study is to ensure the reliability of the instrument used. The analysis was conducted for each of the constructs and its dimensions. SPSS package (Version 26) was used to run the pilot test. During the pilot test stage, convergent and discriminant validity was not conducted. The convergent and discriminant validity will be conducted using the PLS-SEM procedure in the measurement model for formative and reflective in the final data collection phase. It was not practical to conduct it during the pilot test due to the small sample size.

The pilot test result shows an excellent reliability coefficient of variables for the instrument. The coefficient's value was above the minimum acceptable level of 0.7, as suggested by Sekaran (2010). Cronbach's alpha was applied to test reliability with the following results (Table 7.14). While Table 7.15 shows the profile of the respondents for pilot test.

The measurement items are reliable and able to proceed for full data collection based on the pilot test result. New data set will be used for the data analysis.

Administering the Survey (Data Collection)

Administering the survey is one of the essential steps of data collection (Chua, 2003). Data was collected personally by the researcher with support from the HLSP. The questionnaires were distributed using online submission in the identified HLSP. Adequate time was given for the respondent to complete the questionnaire online. This is to ensure a high response rate. Before data entry, all questionnaires were

Table 7.14 Cronbach's Alpha

No	Variables	Cronbach's Alpha (α)	No. of Items	Clarification
1	Asset specificity	0.907	6	Strongly good
2	Barriers	0.817	10	Excellent
3	Commitments	0.808	10	Excellent
4	Halal supply chain integrity	0.845	10	Excellent
5	Quality assurance	0.824	9	Excellent
6	Traceability	0.714	15	Good
7	Trust	0.814	16	Excellent
	Total		76	

Table 7.15 Pilot Test Respondents Profile

Age Group	Frequency	Percent (%)
21–35	3	10
36–50	22	73
51–65	5	17
65 and above	0	0
Total	30	100
Educational qualifications		
Postgraduate	11	37
Graduate	18	60
Diploma	1	3
Post- secondary	0	0
Total	30	100
Working experience – managerial level		
3 years or less	2	7
4–10 years	7	23
More than ten years	13	43
Less than 20 years	8	27
Total	30	100
Experience sector		
Transportation/ warehouse	12	40
Logistics & supply chain	13	43
Halal Supply Chain	5	17
Others	0	0
Total	30	100
Operation year		
Less than 5	5	17
5–15 years	7	23
16–24 years	14	47
More than 25 years	4	13
Total	30	100

checked for any incomplete, missing, and wrong scale used. Only a complete questionnaire was used for data entry. Data were then keyed in using SPSS version 26. All responses were uniquely coded to ensure better traceability and identification.

This study divided data analysis into two main phases: descriptive and structural equation modelling (SEM). The SEM analysis is divided into measurement model and structural model. The purpose of the measurement model is to assess the reliability and validity of the constructs. Meanwhile, the structural model examines the model's predictive capabilities and the relationship between the constructs.

The present study used Structural equation modelling (SEM) through PLS to study the relationship between different constructs of the conceptual framework and to measure the overall fitness of the structural model (Rönkkö et al., 2016). Two processes are usually involved in SEM-PLS: structural model analysis and measurement model analysis. The present study used the structural model to determine the latent variables' causal relationship and unexplained variance. While the measurement model defines the reliability and validity of the observed variables, it also identifies how latent variables and hypothetical constructs can be measured in terms of observed variables (Ringle et al., 2018). Compared to other techniques like multiple regression and path analysis, SEM-PLS offers many advantages (Ringle et al., 2015). SEM-PLS can assess the reliability of each latent variable. At the same time, path analysis assumes that the used scales and basic constructs are equal (Yahaya et al., 2019). Considering the structural equations, SEM-PLS allows for the modelling of unexplained variance. SEM-PLS also provides the model's overall fit to summarise the complex models.

The Choice PLS (Partial Lease Square) in this Study

PLS has several advantages over other statistical software like AMOS and LISREL. It requires no assumptions about variable distribution and allows a small sample size (Yahaya et al., 2019). Moreover, PLS is effective in situations where the theoretical foundation is explained earlier.

Measurement Model

As prescribed in the literature, the confirmation of a reflective measurement model can be verified by testing its internal consistency, convergent validity and discriminant validity (Straub et al., 2004; Lewis et al., 2005).

Internal Consistency

In the traditional sense, the measurement of internal consistency is the assessment of Cronbach's alpha (CA). Higher values of CA within a construct show that items have a similar range in meaning. This is a method of reliability estimate based on item intercorrelations. In the case of PLS, the evaluation of internal consistency depends on composite reliability (CR) (Chin, 1998). CR determines the outer loadings of items individually because CA underestimates the reliability and assumes it is nonequivalent among measures while weighing all items equally (Werts et al., 1974). In some instances, reliability threshold values lie above 0.7 to 09 or even 1. Values below 0.6 indicate a lack of reliability.

Indicator Reliability

The reliability assessment measures the degree to which a variable is consistently measuring what is intended (Urbach & Ahlemann, 2010). Chin (1998) indicates the values of loading above 0.5 to be significant and greater than 0.7 to be great as they explain the variance up to 50% at that level. Bootstrapping is often employed to test the significance of item loadings. The decision to eliminate an item based on loadings should be taken seriously as it can affect the CR, causing it to decrease along with AVE. This should only be undertaken if reliability is extremely low (Henseler et al., 2009).

Convergent Validity

Convergent validity reflects the convergence of a construct compared to others when an individual item is measuring a construct (Urbach & Ahlemann, 2010). In PLS, convergent validity is measured through the values of AVE. Fornell and Larcker (1981) have indicated adequate convergent validity when a construct has an AVE value of at least 0.5.

Discriminant Validity

Discriminant validity is a measure of differentiating items of a construct from another construct in the model. It determines whether the items unintentionally measure what they are not supposed to gauge (Urbach and Ahlemann, 2010). In PLS, three approaches are used for this purpose, i.e. Fornell and Larcker criteria (1981), Cross loadings (Chin, 1998) and HTMT ratio of correlations.

Cross loadings are obtained through correlations of every LV score compared to all other component scores (Chin, 1998). The item loading is observed, and if for a designated construct it appears to be the highest for a designated construct from all other constructs, it is inferred that the indicators are non-exchangeable.

Fornell-Larcker's criterion assumes an LV exhibits more variance within its allocated items than other variables. The AVE of a construct must be larger than the square root of correlations with every other variable.The review of validation rules to assess a reflective measurement model is listed in Table 7.16.

Hence, in this analysis, the measurement model's validity is acceptable when:

1 CR > 0.8.
2 Item's loading >0.7 also significant <0.05.
3 AVE >0.50.
4 Outer loading of every item is greatest for its assigned construct.
5 The square root of the AVE of a construct > correlations between all other constructs in the model.

Structural Model

Assessment of structural model supports the hypotheses through data for a research model the assessment is done after satisfactory outcomes

Table 7.16 Summaries of Validity Guidelines for Assessing Reflective Measurement Model

No	Validity Type	Criterion	Guidelines
1	Internal consistency	CR	CR >0.70
2	Indicator reliability	Indicator loadings	Items loading >0.70 and significant at least at the 0.05 level
	Convergent validity	AVE Cross loadings	AVE >0.50 Item's loading of each indicator is highest for its designated construct
3	Discriminant validity	Fornell and Larcker	The square root of the AVE of a construct should be greater than the correlations between the constructs in the mode
4		HTMT	HTMT is below cut off value of 0.85

of measurement model assessment (Urbach & Ahlemann, 2010). The structural model is assessed using path coefficients and coefficients of determination R^2.

One of the main criteria for PLS structural model assessment is the evaluation of R^2, which calculates the relationship of the latent variable's variance (explained) to its total variance. Chin (1998) has indicated the values of R^2 around 0.6 to be substantial, with lower values around 0.3 to be moderate and 0.1 to be considered weak. However, the literature establishes that the criteria for judging R^2 values depend upon the discipline in which the research is being conducted.

The study of path coefficients allows the researcher to determine the strength of the relationship among variables. T- statistics and significance values are crucial in determining the relevance of the model and relationships within. Huber (2007) has indicated that path coefficient values of 0.1 and above and a level of significance below 0.5 signify impactful relationships in the model.

Hence, in this analysis, the structural model is assessed by:

- Path coefficient between LVs must be at least 0.1 and significant <0.05.
- T-statistics values >1.96

Summary of Data Analysis (Table 7.17)

Table 7.17 Summaries of Data Analysis

Step 1	Measurement Model	Remarks
Step 1.1	Model reliability	
	• Outer loadings	0.70 or higher is preferred. If it is exploratory research, 0.4 or higher is acceptable. (Hulland, 1999)
	• Individual item reliability	A Cronbach's alpha of .70 and above is good, .80 and above is much better, and .90 and above is best (Shemwell et al., 2015)
	• Composite reliability	Composite reliability should be 0.7 or higher. If it is exploratory research, 0.6 or higher is acceptable. (Bagozzi & Yi, 1988)
	• Average Variance • Extracted (AVE)	It should be 0.5 or higher (Bagozzi & Yi, 1988)

(Continued)

Step 1	*Measurement Model*	*Remarks*
Step 1.2	Discriminant validity	
	• Fornell-Larcker	Fornell and Larcker (1981) suggest that the "square root" of AVE of each latent variable should be greater than correlations among the latent variables
	• Cross Loadings	HTMT<0.85
		HTMT<0.90
		(Chin & Newsted 1999)
	• HTMT	HTMT inference using bootstrapping technique: Does 90% bootstrap confidence interval of HTMT include the value of 1<HTMT< (Liberal Criterion)
Step 2	Structural model	
	Path coefficients of the research hypotheses	p-value <0.05 t value >1.96 (Hair Jr et al., 2016)
	Coefficients of determination (R^2)	R^2 evaluate the combined effect of exogenous variables on endogenous latent variables. Where 0.75, 0.50, 0.25, respectively, describe substantial, moderate, or weak levels of predictive accuracy (Hair Jr et al., 2016)
	Model fit	SRMR <0.08 and NFI >0.90 A value less than 0.10 or 0.08 (in a more conservative version; see Hu and Bentler, 1999) is considered a good fit. The closer the NFI to 1, the better the fit.

Measurement Model Assessment

The measuring model was evaluated using the Smart PLS version 3 to analyze over 60 items based on a 5-point Likert scale. These measured elements have been loaded under their respective construct.

The constructs and items were evaluated with average variance (AVE) extracted, discrimination in validity, reliability, and model coefficients. Halal supply chain integrity was the dependent variable in this study. The independent variables are halal traceability, halal assets specificity, halal quality assurance, trust; commitment as mediator and barriers as moderator towards the halal supply chain's dependent variable. The item measured of each variable is labelled as stated in Figure 7.1. Halal supply chain integrity was the dependent variable in this study. The independent variables are halal traceability (TRC), halal assets specificity (AS), halal quality assurance (QA), trust (TR). Commitment (CMT) as mediator and barriers (BAR) as moderator towards the Halal supply chain's dependent variable. The item measured of each variable is labelled as stated in Figure 7.1.

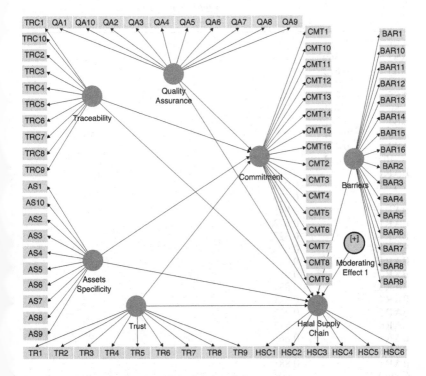

Figure 7.1 Hypothesized model of the study

Indicator: TRC, Traceability; AS, Asset Specificity; QA, Quality Assurance; TR, Trust; CMT, Commitment; Barriers, BAR and HSCI-Halal Supply Chain Integrity

Evaluation of Measurement Model

The main analysis was conducted using PLS-SEMS (partial-least square structural equation modelling) that utilised SmartPLS 3 software package. The first analysis was the measurement model for the first stage of the analysis before continuing with the structural model (Anderson & Gerbing, 1988).

The analysis entails an assessment of the reliability and validity of the relationship between variables and constructs. This study had conducted the required assessments on reliability and validity of the measurement model, namely the internal consistency of coefficient

Table 7.18 Items Outer Loading Reflective Constructs

	Assets Specificity	Barriers	Commitment	Halal Supply Chain	Quality Assurance	Traceability	Trust
AS1	0.814						
AS2	0.569						
AS3	0.812						
AS4	0.847						
AS5	0.763						
AS6	0.742						
AS7	0.787						
AS8	0.754						
AS9	0.495						
AS10	0.473						
BAR1		0.914					
BAR10		0.938					
BAR11		0.925					
BAR12		0.945					
BAR13		0.873					
BAR14		0.827					
BAR15		0.026					
BAR16		0.047					
BAR2		0.913					
BAR3		0.839					
BAR4		0.815					
BAR5		0.927					
BAR6		0.872					
BAR7		0.866					
BAR8		0.885					
BAR9		0.888					
CMT1			0.680				
CMT10			0.932				
CMT11			0.932				
CMT12			0.840				
CMT13			0.849				

	Barriers	Commitment	Halal Supply Chain	Quality Assurance	Traceability	Trust
Assets Specificity						
CMT14			0.845			
CMT15			0.800			
CMT16			0.876			
CMT2				0.654		
CMT3				0.578		
CMT4				0.698		
CMT5				0.806		
CMT6				0.865		
CMT7				0.868		
CMT8				0.841		
CMT9				0.861		
HSC1					0.875	
HSC2					0.923	
HSC3					0.919	
HSC4					0.890	
HSC5					0.666	
HSC6					0.787	
QA1						0.697
QA10						0.887
QA2						0.758
QA3						0.895
QA4						0.906
QA5						0.890
QA6						0.925
QA7						0.910
QA8						0.884
QA9						0.876
TR1						0.883
TR2						0.786
TR3						0.723
TR4						0.816
TR5						0.814
TR6						0.843
TR7						0.808
TR8						0.686
TR9						0.821
TRC1					0.632	
TRC10					0.814	
TRC2					0.580	
TRC3					0.653	
TRC4					0.497	
TRC5					0.592	
TRC6					0.677	
TRC7					0.716	
TRC8					0.591	
TRC9					0.788	

Source: SmartPLS analysis output

alpha and the composite reliability, indicator reliability, convergent validity of AVE, as well as the discriminant validity by examining the cross-loading of indicators and Fornell Larker's criterion (Fornell & Larcker, 1981; Ghozali & Latan, 2015; Hair et al., 2017).

Table 7.18 shows the key indicators of the Latent variable towards the observed variables. The value indicated how much each observable variable or item contributes absolutely to the definition of the latent variable. Outer loading relevance testing is carried out based on the following criteria. If outer loading is less than 0.4, the reflective indicator is deleted. Suppose the outer loading is less than 0.7 but greater than 0.4. In that case, the impact of indicator deletion on AVE and the composite reliability is analysed. The indicator is deleted if the deletion increases the measures above the threshold. On the other view, Hulland (1999) recommended that the value of less than 0.5 be removed. It was also suggested that any value of item loadings is acceptable unless CR and AVE are not affected. In other words, if CR is more than 0.70 and AVE is more than 0.5. (Sutton et al., 2018). However, it should not be less than 0.40 (Joseph F. Hair et al., 2019).

In this research, the initial AVE was between 0.436–0.719. Based on that, weak indicators must be removed from the model or not included in subsequent tests to improve each item's measurement score (external loading) (Sutton et al., 2018). For this study, the cut-off value taken for outer loading is 0.5. An iterative process is adopted to eliminate the manifest variables by considering the suggestions of Sarstedt et al. (2014). The next step is to repeat the validity of each item to meet the rule of thumb that has been set (Table 7.19).

Table 7.19 Revised Items Outer

	Assets Specificity	Barriers	Commitment	Halal Supply Chain	Quality Assurance	Traceability	Trust
AS1	0.853						
AS2	0.849						
AS3	0.882						
AS4	0.727						
AS5	0.794						
AS6	0.828						
AS7	0.810						
BAR1		0.915					
BAR10		0.938					
BAR11		0.925					
BAR12		0.945					
BAR13		0.875					

	Assets Specificity	*Barriers*	*Commitment*	*Halal Supply Chain*	*Quality Assurance*	*Traceability*	*Trust*
BAR14		0.828					
BAR2		0.913					
BAR3		0.841					
BAR4		0.818					
BAR5		0.927					
BAR6		0.871					
BAR7		0.865					
BAR8		0.883					
BAR9		0.886					
CMT10			0.950				
CMT11			0.956				
CMT12			0.891				
CMT13			0.894				
CMT14			0.839				
CMT15			0.854				
CMT16			0.883				
CMT5			0.767				
CMT6			0.886				
CMT7			0.888				
CMT8			0.791				
CMT9			0.911				
HSC1				0.900			
HSC2				0.937			
HSC3				0.928			
HSC4				0.902			
HSC6				0.755			
QA10						0.902	
QA2						0.712	
QA3						0.913	
QA4						0.910	
QA5					0.892		
QA6					0.928		
QA7					0.907		
QA8					0.902		
QA9					0.895		
TR1							0.879
TR2							0.780
TR3							0.744
TR4							0.813
TR5							0.833
TR6							0.828
TR7							0.802
TR9							0.828
TRC10					0.956		
TRC6					0.743		
TRC9					0.918		

Internal Consistency

Internal consistency was the first criterion to be assessed. The measurement model conducted two internal consistency tests to measure the construct's reliability.

Cronbach's Alpha

Cronbach's alpha or Coefficient alpha (alpha) was the first internal consistency test. Cronbach's alpha was used to calculate the internal reliability of each variable. According to Hair et al. (2014), Cronbach's alpha function assumes an equal load of indicators and represents a conservative internal consistency measure. According to Table 7.20 and Figure 7.2, Cronbach's alpha values ranged from 0.846 to 0.979.

Cronbach's alpha measure of internal consistency: how closely related a set of items are as a group. It is considered to be a measure of scale reliability. The result of the alpha coefficient, as shown

Table 7.20 Cronbach's Alpha Value

No	Constructs	Cronbach's Alpha
1	Traceability	0.846
2	Assets specificity	0.919
3	Quality assurance	0.965
4	Trust	0.927
5	Commitment	0.972
6	Halal supply chain	0.931
7	Barriers	0.979

Source: SmartPLS output

No	Constructs	Cronbach's Alpha
1	Traceability	0.846
2	Assets Specificity	0.919
3	Quality Assurance	0.965
4	Trust	0.927
5	Commitment	0.972
6	Halal Supply Chain	0.931
7	Barriers	0.979

Figure 7.2 Cronbach's alpha

in Table 7.20, suggests that the items have relatively high internal consistency. a reliability coefficient of.70 or higher is considered "acceptable" in most social science research situations.

Composite Reliability

Composite reliability was achieved as a further test of reliability was carried out. Higher composite reliability values indicate a higher level of reliability, ranging from 0 to 1, Hair et al., 2017. Composite reliability values in this study ranged from 0.908 to 0.981. The reliability higher than 0.9 is regarded as excellent, higher than 0.8 is fine, higher than 0.7 is adequate, higher than 0.6 is doubtful, and lower than 0.5 is substandard (Joseph F. Hair & Fávero, 2019)

Regarding the inner model assessment on reliability and validity, this study further examined composite reliability (Jöreskog, 1971) of a construct as a precondition in confirming the convergent validity.

Table 7.21 Composite Reliability Value

No	Constructs	Composite Reliability
	Traceability	0.908
2	Assets specificity	0.936
3	Quality assurance	0.971
4	Trust	0.940
5	Commitment	0.976
6	Halal supply chain	0.948
7	Barriers	0.981

Source: SmartPLS output

No	Constructs	Composite Reliability
1	Traceability	0.908
2	Assets Specificity	0.936
3	Quality Assurance	0.971
4	Trust	0.940
5	Commitment	0.976
6	Halal Supply Chain	0.948
7	Barriers	0.981

Figure 7.3 Composite reliability of variables

The outcome of composite reliability of constructs used in this study showed a good and acceptable range of more than 0.7 (Ali et al., 2018; Ghozali & Latan, 2015; Hair et al., 2017) for confirmatory research (Ali et al., 2018; Hair et al., 2017; Latan & Ramli, 2013). Table 7.21 and Figure 7.3 summarises the outcome of the measurement model of composite reliability.

Convergent Validity through AVE

Hair et al. (2017) claimed that "convergent validity refers to the degree of multiple items correlates positively with another measured item of the same construct." Hair et al. (2017) also stated that researchers "should consider the external loads of indicators and average variance extracted (AVE) in assessing the convergent validity of the meaning building." Therefore, it was recommended by Hair et al. (2017) that "each latent construct's AVE should be 0.50 or higher." Hair et al. (2017) further explained that the "AVE value of 0.50 or higher indicates that the construct defines an average of more than half of the indicator's variance." It is commonly assessed through the average variance extracted (AVE). In this study, the AVE values Traceability (0.770), Assets Specificity (0.675), Quality Assurance (0.786), Trust (0.663), Commitment (0.770), HSC (0.787), show that all the values were above the minimum necessary 0.50 as shown in Table 7.22. Based on the result, it is confirmed that this analysis compromises high levels of convergent validity. Figure 7.4 show the validation of measurement.

Discriminant Validity

Discriminant validity is the extent of differentiation of one construct from another in an empirical sense (Hair et al., 2014). Various methods

Table 7.22 AVE (Average Variance Extracted) of Reflective Constructs

No	Constructs	Extracted (AVE)
1	Traceability	0.770
2	Assets specificity	0.675
3	Quality assurance	0.786
4	Trust	0.663
5	Commitment	0.770
6	Halal supply chain	0.787
7	Barriers	0.790

Source: SmartPLS output

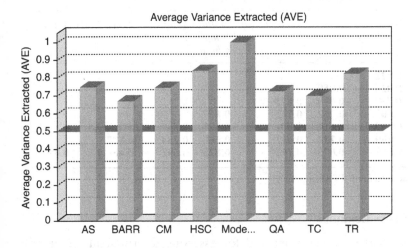

Figure 7.4 AVE (Average Variance Extracted)

have been identified in the literature for the evaluation of discriminant validity. The three most popular methods are the Fornell-Larcker criterion, cross-loadings, and Heterotrait Monotrait (HTMT) correlation ratio.

Fornell-Lacker Criterion

This method to evaluate discriminant validity involves the comparison of the square the root of AVE of the construct with the correlations of all other constructs in the model (Hair et al., 2014). A latent construct should be able to explain its variance better than the variance of another latent construct in the model. This is achieved by calculating the square root of the variance of each construct and comparing it with the correlations of other constructs (Anderson & Fornell, 1994). The AVE values are generated using Smart PLS software which calculates the square root of AVE for each construct and exhibits them all in tabular form, which is presented below in Table 7.23. The bold values in the table represent the square root of AVE, and the non- bold values represent the correlations among the constructs. It is clear from the table that all off-diagonal values are lower than the topmost values in the columns. Hence the Fornell-Larcker criterion is met for the discriminant validity of the measurement model.

Table 7.23 Fornell Larker's Criterion

Assets Specificity	Barriers	Commitment	Halal Supply Chain	Quality Assurance	Traceability	Trust
0.822						
−0.028	**0.889**					
0.739	**−0.099**	**0.878**				
0.507	**−0.252**	**0.742**	**0.887**			
0.699	**−0.012**	**0.801**	**0.521**	**0.887**		
0.409	**−0.224**	**0.417**	**0.560**	**0.284**	**0.877**	
0.588	**−0.073**	**0.792**	**0.828**	**0.692**	**0.486**	**0.814**

Source: SmartPLS Output

Cross Loadings

The other common method for assessing discriminant validity is Cross loadings generated by the algorithm in Smart PLS. Table 7.24 generated by Smart PLS exhibits loadings for measurement items for each construct that are higher than other latent variables. The table shows that loading in each block for a specific construct is higher than all other blocks. These values indicate the separation of latent variables as theorized in the conceptual framework of this study. This cross-loading fulfil the second criteria for the discriminant validity of the measurement model in this study.

Table 7.24 Cross Loading

AR14	−0.009	**0.828**	−0.127	−0.196	−0.062	−0.209	−0.100
BAR2	−0.029	**0.913**	−0.101	−0.225	−0.004	−0.127	−0.064
BAR3	−0.153	**0.841**	−0.145	−0.258	−0.074	−0.224	−0.108
BAR4	0.021	**0.818**	0.036	−0.138	0.062	−0.189	−0.016
BAR5	−0.026	**0.927**	−0.079	−0.260	0.013	−0.224	−0.065
BAR6	−0.061	**0.871**	−0.101	−0.214	−0.053	−0.196	−0.064
BAR7	−0.026	**0.865**	−0.115	−0.228	−0.068	−0.231	−0.095
BAR8	−0.078	**0.883**	−0.116	−0.202	−0.077	−0.103	−0.059
BAR9	0.012	**0.886**	−0.094	−0.163	−0.034	−0.204	−0.047
CMT10	0.681	−0.056	**0.950**	0.714	0.762	0.357	0.748
CMT11	0.681	−0.047	**0.956**	0.709	0.763	0.357	0.745
CMT12	0.673	−0.039	**0.891**	0.564	0.788	0.312	0.622
CMT13	0.703	−0.054	**0.894**	0.522	0.826	0.329	0.619
CMT14	0.602	−0.206	**0.839**	0.836	0.569	0.421	0.801
CMT15	0.655	−0.059	**0.854**	0.516	0.767	0.274	0.620
CMT16	0.648	−0.193	**0.883**	0.662	0.767	0.384	0.715

CMT5	0.554	−0.090	**0.767**	0.663	0.569	0.268	0.701
CMT6	0.659	−0.065	**0.886**	0.592	0.705	0.476	0.681
CMT7	0.668	−0.045	**0.888**	0.588	0.712	0.334	0.632
CMT8	0.532	−0.067	**0.791**	0.774	0.498	0.431	0.788
CMT9	0.721	−0.100	**0.911**	0.604	0.724	0.421	0.616
HSC1	0.510	−0.343	0.715	**0.900**	0.560	0.497	0.760
HSC2	0.515	−0.255	0.709	**0.937**	0.490	0.487	0.741
HSC3	0.584	−0.208	0.751	**0.928**	0.560	0.505	0.799
HSC4	0.414	−0.216	0.625	**0.902**	0.409	0.480	0.689
HSC6	0.186	−0.077	0.463	**0.755**	0.260	0.519	0.675
QA10	0.627	−0.065	0.667	0.402	**0.902**	0.189	0.551
QA2	0.461	−0.037	0.574	0.493	**0.712**	0.460	0.598
QA3	0.678	−0.023	0.799	0.532	**0.913**	0.176	0.678
QA4	0.599	−0.075	0.778	0.599	**0.910**	0.234	0.693
QA5	0.577	0.096	0.627	0.280	**0.892**	0.188	0.500
QA6	0.634	0.009	0.688	0.369	**0.928**	0.253	0.569
QA7	0.632	−0.002	0.736	0.461	**0.907**	0.353	0.665
QA8	0.681	0.027	0.718	0.422	**0.902**	0.134	0.525
QA9	0.664	−0.001	0.747	0.519	**0.895**	0.293	0.687
TR1	0.418	−0.006	0.563	0.713	0.434	0.481	**0.879**
TR2	0.337	−0.087	0.530	0.680	0.374	0.513	**0.780**
TR3	0.601	−0.090	0.724	0.617	0.542	0.324	**0.744**
TR4	0.444	−0.134	0.611	0.732	0.563	0.611	**0.813**
TR5	0.710	−0.088	0.862	0.659	0.847	0.296	**0.833**
TR6	0.337	0.030	0.535	0.643	0.492	0.356	**0.828**
TR7	0.393	−0.075	0.549	0.631	0.531	0.228	**0.802**
TR9	0.515	−0.014	0.710	0.710	0.647	0.359	**0.828**
TRC10	0.391	−0.240	0.417	0.552	0.232	**0.956**	0.468
TRC6	0.300	−0.220	0.325	0.379	0.376	**0.743**	0.381
TRC9	0.379	−0.136	0.349	0.526	0.175	**0.918**	0.427

Source: SmartPLS analysis output

Heterotrait-Monotrait (HTMT) Ratio of Correlation

The third most recent measure for discriminant validity is the HTMT ratio of correlations. The values range from 0 to 1 but closer to 1 values are considered a lack of discriminant validity. However, some authors have suggested an upper threshold of 0.85 (Kline, 2011) and a value of 0.9 (Gold et al., 2001). Table 7.25 below show that HTMT values are well below the prescribed.

Overall, the tests for reliability and validity of the measurement model in this study have been confirmed and state that the study can proceed to assess the structural model.

Table 7.25 Heterotraut Monotrait Ratio (HTMT)

Assets Specificity	Barriers	Commitment	Halal Supply Chain	Quality Assurance	Traceability
0.095					
0.779	0.108				
0.540	0.253	0.770			
0.739	0.070	0.823	0.534		
0.464	0.247	0.458	0.628	0.333	
0.627	0.090	0.819	0.841	0.713	**0.550**

Source: SmartPLS Output

Analysis

The next step is to display the hypothesized relationship among the tested variables through the PLS Algorithm using Partial Least Square Structural Equation. The research used the standard bootstrapping technique with 5000 samples and 101 cases in the data set to measure the importance of the direct relationship route coefficient. The structural model directly relates Traceability, Asset Specificity, Quality Assurance, Trust, Commitment and Halal Supply Chain Integrity.

Structural Model Analysis

Assessment of structural model supports the hypotheses through data for a research model the assessment is done after satisfactory outcomes of the measurement model assessment (Urbach & Ahlemann, 2010). The structural model is assessed using the path coefficients and coefficients of determination R^2.

One of the main criteria for PLS structural model assessment is the evaluation of R^2, which calculates the relationship of the latent variable's variance (explained) to its total variance. Chin (1998) has indicated the values of R^2 around 0.6 to be substantial, with lower values around 0.3 to be moderate and 0.1 to be considered weak. The literature however, it establishes that the criteria for judging R^2 values depend upon the discipline in which the research is being conducted.

The study of path coefficients allows the researcher to determine the strength of the relationship among variables. T-statistics and significance values are crucial in determining the relevance of the model and relationships within. Huber (2007) has indicated that path coefficient values of 0.1 and above and level of significance below 0.5 signify impactful relationships in the model. Table 7.26 below condenses the standards for structural model assessment.

For path coefficient, the value of β 0.02 is small, β 0.15 as a medium, and β 0.35 as large (Cohen, 1988). Some values had set the lowest threshold of 0.05 as significant (Urbach & Ahlemann, 2010). In addition, t-value and p-value are referred to using bootstrapping procedure to determine the significance of the path coefficient. The cut-off values of t- values >1.96 (5% confidence level) and p-value <0.05 denote the path is significant (Hair et al., 2017). The effect size value R^2 0.25, > 0.25 < 0.5 and > 0.5 indicate the effect size of weak, moderate, and high, respectively (Ghozali & Latan, 2015). Each assessment result is presented in the next sub-headings.

Collinearity Assessment

Assessment on collinearity issues should be conducted beforehand in determining that the constructs and items in the model did not suffer from multicollinearity. Highly inter-associating an independent variable may distort the data and cause statistical inference that may lead to unreliable data (Hair et al., 2014). Hence, the variance inflated factor (VIF) values are used in determining the level of collinearity between constructs (Hair et al., 2017).

Constructs should be within the range of acceptable VIF values aforementioned. Tables 7.27–7.33 shows the inner model collinearity assessment result between all relationship paths of independent and dependent variables. For the hypothesized model, the relationship paths can be segregated into three sets:

- Assessment between all independent variables (AS, QA, TC & TR) and the dependent variable of HSC (Halal Supply Chain);
- Assessment between independent variables and the mediator variable of commitments);

Table 7.26 Inner Model Collinearity Assessment

First set IVs→DV		Second set IVs→Mediator		Third set Mediator→DV	
Construct	VIF	Construct	VIF	Construct	VIF
AS	2.178	AS	2.574	Halal	2.722
QA	2.671	QA	2.238	supply	
TC	1.407	TC	1.530	Chain	
TR	2.344	TR	2.114		

Source: Own study. SmartPLS analysis output

- Evaluation between the mediator (CM and the dependent variable (HSC).

Various recommendations for acceptable levels of VIF have been published in the literature. Perhaps most commonly, a value of 10 has been recommended as the maximum level of VIF (Hair et al., 1995; Kennedy, 1992; Marquardt, 1970; Neter, Wasserman, & Kutner, 1989).

The VIF recommendation of 10 corresponds to the tolerance recommendation of.10 (i.e., 1/10 = 10). However, a recommended maximum VIF value of 5 (Rogerson, 2001) and even 4 (Pan & Jackson, 2008) can be found in the literature. VIF > 5 is cause for concern, and VIF > 10 indicates a serious collinearity problem (Menard S. 2001).

Table 7.26 shows that the inner model does not suffer from collinearity issues where the VIFs for all constructs ranges between 1.407 to 2.671.

Table 7.27 Summarised Result on Path Coefficient's of Direct Relationship Between IVs and DV Using Bootstrapping Procedure

Original Sample (O)	Sample Mean (M)	Standard Deviation (STDEV)	T Statistics (|O/STDEV|)	P Value
0.169	0.182	0.081	2.088	0.037
−0.080	−0.086	0.083	0.967	**0.333**
−0.233	−0.199	0.170	1.368	**0.171**
0.603	0.564	0.148	4.085	0.000
0.023	0.045	0.074	0.310	**0.756**
0.260	0.245	0.097	2.685	0.007
0.342	0.325	0.100	3.432	0.001
0.391	0.400	0.105	3.704	0.000
0.412	0.415	0.177	2.327	0.020

Source: SmartPLS output.

Table 7.28 Summarised Result on the Role of Mediator Between IVs and DV

Original Sample (O)	Sample Mean (M)	Standard Deviation (STDEV)	T Statistics (|O/STDEV|)	P Value
0.107	0.100	0.058	1.843	**0.065**
0.141	0.139	0.082	1.718	**0.086**
0.009	0.020	0.035	0.269	**0.788**
0.161	0.164	0.082	1.966	0.049

Table 7.29 Summarized Result on Path Coefficient's of Asset Specificity

Original Sample (O)	Sample Mean (M)	Standard Deviation (STDEV)	T Statistics (|O/STDEV|)	P Value
−0.080	−0.086	0.083	0.967	**0.333**
0.260	0.245	0.097	2.685	0.007
0.107	0.100	0.058	1.843	**0.065**

Table 7.30 Summarized Result on Path Coefficient's of Quality Assurance

Original Sample (O)	Sample Mean (M)	Standard Deviation (STDEV)	T Statistics (|O/STDEV|)	P Value
−0.233	−0.199	0.170	1.668	**0.171**
0.342	0.325	0.100	3.432	0.001
0.141	0.139	0.082	1.718	**0.086**

Table 7.31 Summarized Result on Path Coefficient's of Traceability

Original Sample (O)	Sample Mean (M)	Standard Deviation (STDEV)	T Statistics (|O/STDEV|)	P Value
0.169	0.182	0.081	2.088	0.037
0.023	0.045	0.074	0.310	**0.756**
0.009	0.020	0.035	0.269	**0.788**

Table 7.32 Summarized Result on Path Coefficient's of Trust

Original Sample (O)	Sample Mean (M)	Standard Deviation (STDEV)	T Statistics (|O/STDEV|)	P Value
0.603	0.564	0.148	4.085	0.007
0.391	0.400	0.105	3.704	0.008
0.161	0.184	0.082	1.966	0.049

Table 7.33 Summarized Result on Path Coefficient's of Moderating Effect

Original Sample (O)	Sample Mean (M)	Standard Deviation (STDEV)	T Statistics (|O/STDEV|)	P Value
0.090	0.089	0.056	1.605	**0.109**

Path Coefficient Assessment on Relationships Between Constructs

The next assessment is to estimate the structural model regarding the hypothesized relationships between the constructs in the study. The path coefficient estimates are produced after running the PLS-SEM algorithm to determine the strength of relationships. A standard path coefficient interpretation examines the β value of path coefficient between -1 to 1, in which the value closer to 0 denotes diminishing significance (Cohen, 1988; Hair et al., 2017).

For path coefficient estimates, it is crucial to establish that the values are significant, which reflect the relationship of constructs. Therefore, the assessment that includes standard coefficient error is conducted using the bootstrapping procedure in SmartPLS. The output of t-value and p-value will reveal its significance if the t-value is more than 1.96 (significant level = 5%) and the p-value is less than 0.05 (Hair et al., 2017).

According to the hypothesized model, this study assessed seven direct relationships. The first direct relationships are between the independent variables (AS, QA, TC & TR) and Halal Supply Chain (HSC). The second set is between the independent variables (AS, QA, TC & TR) and the intervening variable of CM (commitments).

Additionally, the direct relationship of CM and HSC is reported in separate sub- headings that include a complete assessment in determining the mediation role of CM on the path relationship between IVs and DV.

Relationship of Independent Variables (AS, QA, TC & TR) and Dependent Variable (HSC)

Table 7.27 summarizes the result for the hypotheses. Traceability ($\beta = 0.169$, $p < 0.05$) was significant predictors of Halal supply chain. Asset specificity ($\beta = -0.080$, $p > 0.05$) and quality assurance ($\beta = -0.233$, $p > 0.05$) were found to be negatively significant towards Halal supply chain. Apart from that, traceability ($\beta = 0.023$, $p = < 0.005$) was significantly towards the Halal supply chain. The results indicated that H1 and H4 are supported while H2 and H3 are rejected.

It was also revealed that asset specificity ($\beta = 0.260$, $p < 0.01$), quality assurance ($\beta = 0.342$, $p < 0.01$) and trust ($\beta = 0.391$, $p = < 0.001$) were found to be significantly towards commitment and supports H6, H7 and H8. However, traceability ($\beta = 0.023$, $p > 0.01$), was found not to be a significant predictors thus H4 is rejected. The result also shows that commitment ($\beta = 0.412$, $p = < 0.05$) is a significant predictor towards Halal supply chain and therefore H13 is supported.

The following Figures 7.5 and 7.6 illustrates the hypotheses based on the statistical values as displayed in Table 7.27.

Direct Relationship of Independent Variables (AS, QA, TC & TR) and Commitments (CM)

This assessment focuses on the indirect relationships between a set of independent variables and the dependent variable through

Hypothesis		Original Sample	Sample Mean	Standard Deviation	T Statistics	P Values
H1	Traceability → Halal Supply Chain	0.169	0.182	0.081	2.088	0.037
H2	Assets Specificity → Halal Supply Chain	−0.080	−0.086	0.083	0.967	0.333
H3	Quality Assurance → Halal Supply Chain	−0.233	−0.199	0.170	1.368	0.171
H4	Trust → Halal Supply Chain	0.603	0.564	0.148	4.085	0.000
H5	Traceability → Commitment	0.023	0.045	0.074	0.310	0.756
H6	Assets Specificity → Commitment	0.260	0.245	0.097	2.685	0.007
H7	Quality Assurance → Commitment	0.342	0.325	0.100	3.432	0.001
H8	Trust → Commitment	0.391	0.400	0.105	3.704	0.000
H9	Traceability → Commitment → Halal Supply Chain	0.009	0.020	0.035	0.269	0.788
H10	Assets Specificity → Commitment → Halal Supply Chain	0.107	0.100	0.058	1.843	0.065
H11	Quality Assurance → Commitment → Halal Supply Chain	0.141	0.139	0.082	1.718	0.086
H12	Trust → Commitment → Halal Supply Chain	0.161	0.164	0.082	1.966	0.049
H13	Commitment → Halal Supply Chain	0.412	0.415	0.177	2.327	0.020
H14	Moderating Effect → Halal Supply Chain	0.090	0.089	0.056	1.605	0.109

Figure 7.5 Summary of path coefficients

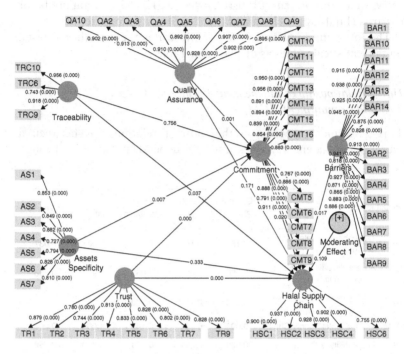

Figure 7.6 Structural Model for Direct Relationships between IVs and DV
Source: Own study. SmartPLS output.

a mediator variable. The role of commitment as a mediator was hypothesised as a variable that measures the relational outcome. The assessment followed the mediation test as suggested by Hair et al. (2017), Hayes (2018), Zhao et al. (2010), and in determining the specific indirect path, total indirect and direct path significance using a boot-strapping procedure.

Table 7.28 derived from the indirect relationship result from Smart PLS. The results revealed that only trust ($\beta = 0.161$, $p < 0.05$) was mediated by commitment. There were found no mediator effect for asset specificity ($\beta = 0.107$, $p > 0.05$), quality assurance ($\beta = 0.141$, $p > 0.086$) and treacability ($\beta = 0.09$, $p > 0.788$).

The result shows that the direct relationship between asset specificity towards Halal supply chain was not significant ($t = 0.967$, $p > 0.05$) but the direct relationship from asset specificity towards commitments was significant (t = 2.685, p < 0.05), and the indirect relationship between asset specificity towards Halal supply chain lead to an insignificant relationship. Such results indicated no mediation role between asset specificity and Halal supply chains. Thus H9 is rejected.

The result of the direct relationship of quality assurance towards the Halal supply chain was found to be insignificant (β = −0.233, p > 0.171); however, the result towards commitment was found to be significant (β = 0.342, p <0.05). The role of commitment as a mediator was insignificant between quality assurance and Halal supply chain (β = 0.141, p > 0.086). There are no mediation effects recorded between quality assurance and the Halal supply chain. Thus H10 is rejected.

A significant relationship is recorded for the direct relationship between traceability towards Halal Supply Chain (β = 0.169, p < 0.037). However, the analysis revealed that the relationship between traceability and commitment was insignificant (β = 0.023, p > 0.756). At the same time, commitments were insignificant in the relationship between traceability and the Halal Supply Chain (β = 0.009, p > 0.788). Such a result indicated no mediation effect in the relationship between traceability and Halal Supply Chain. Thus H11 is rejected.

Direct relationship between trust towards Halal Supply Chain (β = 0.603, p < 0.05) and commitments (β = 0.391, p < 0.05) were found to be significant. The mediation test was also found to be significant (β = 0.161, p < 0.049). such results indicate that commitments mediate partially between trust and the Halal supply chain, and the hypothesis H12 is accepted.

Moderating Effect of Barriers Between Commitments and Halal Supply Chain

Finally, the hypothesis seeks to ascertain the moderating role of barriers between commitments and the Halal supply chain (β = 0.090, p > 0.109). The result indicated that barriers were not a significant moderator in the relationship between commitment and the Halal supply chain. Thus H 14 is rejected.

Figure 7.7 was generated by the SmartPLS from the product indicator approach (a typical moderator analysis results representation uses simple slope plots) and shows that barriers increase the negative effect (Becker et al., 2018; Joseph F. Hair et al., 2021) of commitments and the halal supply chain.

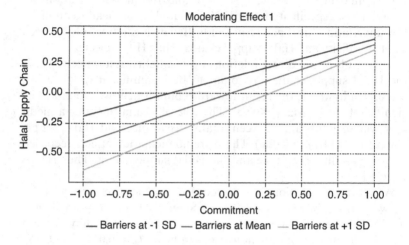

Figure 7.7 Moderator indicator approach

Coefficient of Determinant (R^2)

The R-square (R^2) assessment determines the model's predictive power between certain endogenous constructs linked with the exogenous construct(s). The model's predictive power measurement is based on the squared correlation calculated between the actual and predicted values.

The assessment includes all the data used for model estimation in determining the model's predictive power (Hair et al., 2017; Sarstedt et al., 2014). The coefficient of determination values in the range of 0–1 demonstrates the percentage of predictive accuracy. The values closer to 1 indicate an increasing predictive power and vice versa.

No general rules are established for evaluating the predictive power based on coefficient values, and the interpretation relies on the domain of study (Hair et al., 2017). The suggestion by Henseler et al. (2009) and Hair, Anderson, Tatham, and Black (2010) from the marketing research standpoint classified the value of $0.5 < R_2 > 0.75$ as a medium, and low $0.25 < R_2 < 0.5$ as small predictive power. Other consumer behaviour studies considered the R_2 value of 0.2 as high (Hair, Hult, Ringle, & Sarstedt, 2016), and it depends on the complexity of the model (Hair et al., 2017).

Hair et al. (2017) suggested this study examined the R_2 adjusted in evaluating the model's predictive power by considering the tendency of having insignificant exogeneous in predicting the exogenous

Table 7.34 Summarized Result on Coefficient of Determination (R^2)

Constructs	R Square	R Square Adjusted	Predictive Accuracy Level
Commitment	0.785	0.773	Strong
Halal supply chain	0.791	0.769	Strong

Source Sarstedt et al. (2016)

due to the differences in the study setting. Also, as a guideline for retaining or omitting insignificant constructs from the model (Hair et al., 2017). Table 7.34 summarises the coefficient of determination R_2 and R_2 adjusted for endogenous constructs as well as additional lower-order constructs. The following results indicated that R_2 for commitment and the Halal supply chain were higher than > 0.75. In other words, it shows that both CM and HSC have a strong predictor accuracy.

The Goodness of Fit (GoF)

The global goodness of fit measurement criteria are applied for this study (Tenenhaus et al., 2004; Henseler & Sarstedt, 2013). The measurement of Goodness of Fit (GoF) primarily focuses on the predictive power of the model and the structural model (Latan & Ramli, 2013).

The objective of measuring the goodness of fit model is to ensure global validation for the partial least squares structural equation modelling model performance for both measurement and structural model on the overall prediction performance of the model (Chin, 2011).

In this study, the Standardized Root Mean Square Residual (SRMR) revealed that the goodness of fit model value is 0.075 for the complete main effects or theory testing, which exceeded the cut-off value of less than 0.008 for the model to achieve the fit of interaction as hypothesised (Hair et al., 2017).

The SRMR is defined as the difference between the observed correlation and the model implied correlation matrix. Thus, it allows assessing the average magnitude of the discrepancies between observed and expected correlations as an absolute measure of (model) fit criterion.

A value less than 0.10 or 0.08 (in a more conservative version; see Hu and Bentler, 1999) is considered a good fit. Henseler et al. (2014) introduce the SRMR as a goodness of fit measure for PLS-SEM that can be used to avoid model misspecification. The SRMR is the difference between the observed correlation, and the model implied correlation matrix. Thus, it allows assessing the average magnitude of the discrepancies between observed and expected correlations as an absolute measure of (model) fit criterion (Table 7.35).

Hypotheses Support

Table 7.36 is the summary of the hypotheses testing. The result revealed that only traceability (H1) and trust (H4) are significant in the direct relationship towards the Halal supply chain. The results also show that H6 (asset specificity), H7 (quality assurances) and H8 (trust) were significant. The direct effect showed that traceability and trust were significant and positively related to Halal Supply Chain. Apart from that, only traceability was insignificant, which led H5 to be rejected. At the same time, H6, H7 and H8 were accepted. H12 is the only supported hypothesis in the mediation testing. Finally, H13 revealed that commitment and Halal supply chain are significant; thus, they are accepted. Details are as per the summary Table 7.36 shown below:

Table 7.35 Goodness Fit

	Saturated Model	Estimated Model
SRMR	0.078	0.079

Table 7.36 Consolidated Result for All Paths of Structural Model

Hypothesis	Original Sample (O)	Sample Mean (M)	Standard Deviation (STDEV)	T Statistics (|O/STDEV|)	P Value
H1	0.169	0.182	0.081	2.088	0.037
H2	−0.080	−0.086	0.083	0.967	0.333
H3	−0.233	−0.199	0.170	1.368	0.171
H4	0.603	0.564	0.148	4.085	0.001
H5	0.023	0.045	0.074	0.310	0.756
H6	0.260	0.245	0.097	2.685	0.007
H7	0.342	0.325	0.100	3.432	0.001
H8	0.391	0.400	0.105	3.704	0.000
H9	0.009	0.020	0.035	0.269	0.788
H10	0.107	0.100	0.058	1.843	0.065
H11	0.141	0.139	0.082	1.718	0.086
H12	0.161	0.164	0.082	1.966	0.049
H13	0.412	0.415	0.177	2.327	0.020
H14	0.090	0.089	0.056	1.605	0.109

Summary

A total of ten hypotheses were developed based on theoretical and conceptual existing literature and prior empirical findings. This study confirmed that seven hypotheses were accepted while the balance hypotheses were rejected (Table 7.37).

Table 7.37 Summary of the Hypothesis

Hypothesis	Statements	Remarks
Hypothesis 1	Traceability has a significant relationship with Halal Supply Chain integrity.	Accepted
Hypothesis 2	Assets Specificity has a significant relationship with Halal Supply Chain integrity.	Rejected
Hypothesis 3	Quality Assurance has a significant relationship with Halal Supply Chain integrity.	Rejected
Hypothesis 4	Trust has a significant relationship with Halal Supply Chain integrity.	Accepted
Hypothesis 5	Traceability has a significant relationship with commitments.	Rejected
Hypothesis 6	Assets Specificity has a significant relationship with commitments.	Accepted
Hypothesis 7	Quality Assurance has a significant relationship with commitments.	Accepted
Hypothesis 8	Trust has a significant relationship with commitments.	Accepted
Hypothesis 9	Commitments mediate the relationship between traceability and Halal supply chain integrity.	Rejected
Hypothesis 10	Commitments mediate the relationship between assets specificity and Halal supply chain integrity.	Rejected
Hypothesis 11	Commitments mediate the relationship between quality assurance and Halal Supply Chain integrity.	Rejected
Hypothesis 12	Commitments mediate the relationship between trust and Halal supply chain integrity.	Accepted
Hypothesis 13	Commitment has a significant relationship with Halal supply chain integrity.	Accepted
Hypothesis 14	Barriers moderate the relationship between commitments and Halal supply chain integrity.	Rejected

Key Conclusion from Malaysia Case Study On HSCI

Based on the previous research on Halal Supply Chain Integrity (HSCI), this study investigated the main factor in determining Halal Supply Chain Integrity: Perspective of Halal Logistics Service Provider (HLSP) in Malaysia. In other words, understanding the determinant of HSCI is the main interest of this research.

There are four main objectives and questions concerning the investigations towards the relationship between Halal Traceability, Halal Assets Specificity, Halal Quality Assurance, Trust, Commitments (MV) and Barriers (MV) towards Halal Supply Chain Integrity. Details of research questions and research objectives are appended below for easy references. The results indicated that four out of 14 hypotheses were rejected. A research framework diagram with significant and insignificant relationships is shown as per the following Figure 7.8. Further discussion on the results will be discussed in detail on the next subtopic (Table 7.38).

Discussion

The direct relationship between Halal Traceability, Halal Assets Specificity, Halal Quality Assurance and Trust towards Halal Supply Chain Integrity. The results indicated that Halal traceability and trust contributes to the positive relationship towards the Halal Supply Chain Integrity. It shows that those two predictors are important

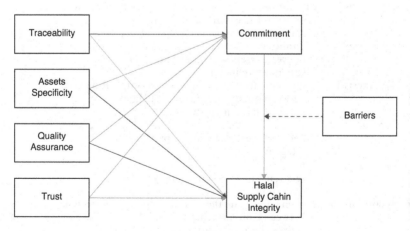

Figure 7.8 Significant and insignificant relationship indicators

Table 7.38 Summary of Research Questions and Research Objectives

Research Questions	Research objectives
Does Halal Traceability, Halal Assets Specificity, Halal Quality Assurance, Trust, and commitments positively affect Halal Supply Chain Integrity?	To determine whether there is a significant direct relationship between Halal Traceability, Halal Assets Specificity, Halal Quality Assurance, Trust and commitments towards Halal Supply Chain Integrity.
Does Halal Traceability, Halal Assets Specificity, Halal Quality Assurance and Trust have a positive relationship towards commitments?	To determine whether there is a significant direct relationship between Halal Traceability, Halal Assets Specificity, Halal Quality Assurance and Trust towards commitments.
Does commitments mediate the relationship between Halal Traceability, Halal Assets Specificity, Halal Quality Assurance and Trust towards Halal Supply Chain Integrity?	To examine whether commitments mediate the relationship between Halal Traceability, Halal Assets Specificity, Halal Quality Assurance and Trust towards Halal Supply Chain Integrity.
Does barriers moderate the relationship between commitments towards Halal Supply Chain Integrity?	To examine whether barriers moderate the relationship between commitments towards Halal Supply Chain Integrity.

to be considered in the Halal Supply Chain Integrity matters. Halal Traceability is important as it reflects the substantial effort towards Halal Traceability.

Halal Traceability in this research can be summarized in three simple functions as follows:

- Ability to track the materials along the supply chain process
- Ability to locate and identify information and history of the supply chain process
- Act as a communication tool to support the tracking purposes along the supply chain process

The role of halal traceability is important. Based on that, the results indicated the significant relationship between halal traceability towards halal supply chain integrity. There will be less effective halal integrity if there is missing track and trace information. Traceability provides transparency and sincereness to all stakeholders in implementing halal integrities, especially to comply with the standards suggested by halal authorities. Such a result supports the previous researchers that presented traceability to be included in further studies of halal integrity (Abd Rahman et al., 2017; Mohamad et al., 2016; Poniman et al., 2014; Saifudin et al., 2018; Zulfakar et al., 2014). This research validates the relationship of traceability statistically for future research references.

Maintaining the integrity of halal products has become a priority for the Malaysian government and consumers. However, there are numerous barriers, misconceptions, and fallacies in the halal supply chain. Some manufacturers and suppliers are unaware of the complexities of handling halal operations. In order to maintain halal integrity, halal production, for example, necessitates Trust and full understanding throughout the supply chain. Furthermore, to conform to Islamic standards, Muslim customers must Trust or be sure that they consume halal, hygienic, and safe. Halal integrity is vital not only for industry players but also for consumer concerns. Based on that, trust can be considered one of the important factors towards integrities. Trust plays an important role as the halal supply chain integrity predictor. The result indicated that trust significantly influences halal supply chain integrity. Such result was parallel with the findings from past studies (Ab Talib & Hamid, 2014; M. H. Ali & Suleiman, 2018; Haleem & Khan, 2017; Tieman, 2011; Zailani et al., 2018). The key to success for the halal supply chain integrity management was stated depending on government support, the existence of certain assets in the form of special assets, information technology support, adequate human resources; vertical and horizontal collaborative relationships, trust, transparency, information disclosure; and finally halal certification. However, the commitments of all stakeholders, especially from the Halal logistic service providers, is really important in realising the integrity issues. A high level of commitment from all the stakeholders is required. It is necessary to complete the Halal process cycle from manufacturer to the end-user. The results were once again validated through statistical evidence of some past suggestions of researchers (Boni & Forleo, 2019; Kottala & Herbert, 2019; Mora-Monge et al., 2019; Selim et al., 2019; Zulfakar et al., 2014).

Asset specificity in this research is based on the service providers willingly investing in their assets to serve the special needs of their partners related to the Halal integration implementation. Although it has been highlighted by a few researchers as a predictor in the halal integrity (Zulfakar et al., 2014), the results were negative. A possible reason for explaining the negative effects is that almost all registered logistics providers have currently utilised modern assets with the help of technology in their business matters regardless of Halal or common supply chain (Ali et al., 2017; Ali & Suleiman, 2018; Hashim & Shariff, 2016; Raut et al., 2019). The asset specificity was becoming needed as the logistics value- added in delivering their services. Based on that, Asset Specificity is becoming non-significant as the service providers already exercise the least requirements as needed by the Halal rules, standards and compliance.

Halal quality assurance refers to the process taken in ensuring the service offered is according to the requirements established by the Halal authorities. The authorisation of Halal service providers went through a strict assessment such as the determination of Halal critical points, verifications on the process flow, evaluation on the control measures and observation on the corrective actions by all the service providers. Standard rules and operational procedures have complied with the Halal supply chain integrity. Halal quality assurance was not significant towards the halal supply chain integrity because those things have been complied with and assessed at the earlier stage before the process of recognition and selection being made by the halal authorities. Those service providers interested in the halal business in the first place must meet the minimum requirements that satisfy the halal standards. Halal quality assurance is not becoming an interesting predictor of the halal integrity examination. Based on the above, the outcome revealed by this study is justified and supported not only by the past literature (Okdinawati et al., 2021; Othman et al., 2016a; Selim et al., 2019) but the industry-standard practice (Sumpin et al., 2019; Yusaini H. et al., 2016).

The Direct Relationship Between Halal Traceability, Halal Assets Specificity, Halal Quality Assurance and Trust Towards Commitments

The direct relationship result reveals that only traceability was not significant towards commitments. An interesting impact was found where traceability was significant towards Halal Supply Chain Integrity but was reported to be insignificant towards commitments. The fact is that traceability has become one of the important elements in the logistics and supply chain industries. From time to time, there are growing concerns about providing additional value to the stakeholders with more information especially related to the track and trace services.

The following statements were taken from various press statements that show traceability has become one of the requirements needed in today's business.

"Consumers want to know they can trust any claims a business is making about a food product being organic, Halal, or part of a sustainable supply chain. And, in a worst-case scenario, they want to know that any food safety notices and product recalls will be handled as transparently and efficiently as possible".

"For the first time, the industry will have an easily accessible methodology that can be used by everyone along the length of the supply chain, enabling information to flow freely regardless of software or technology" (Mccleery, 2021).

Traceability in today contexts related to the logistics and supply chain has become the requirements and standards of service providers. It could be important in the past for compliance purposes (Ab Talib et al., 2015; Haihong et al., 2016; Soon et al., 2017; A. Tan et al., 2018), but today has become a requirement among the players in the industry (Dilla & Fathurohman, 2021). Based on that, it explains why traceability was significant towards Halal Supply Chain Integrity rather than commitments.

Commitments based on past research categorised a few important elements that can be used to summarise and justify the results. Past studies indicate that commitment is related to the willingness and readiness of the service providers and all stakeholders in ensuring (Kristiana et al., 2020; Y. H. Mohamed et al., 2020; Supian et al., 2019; Supian & Abdullah, 2019):

- The commitment of the management in implementing halal logistics
- Required cross-functional commitment by the respective parties
- Visibility and are willing to increase investment based on the special needs
- The willingness to provide dedicated assets to cater for the halal client's requests
- The desire to send the workers to halal training
- The readiness to enhance the integrity of the halal food supply chain
- Play shared roles in protecting and ensuring the halal integrity

Based on the above, it is clear that the implementation of Halal Supply Chain Integrity required a strong commitment to focus on Halal assets specificity, quality assurances and trust. Commitment is needed for Halal Traceability. The absence of commitments will lead to poor facilities or a lack of concerns in the traceability parts (Saleh & Salsabila, 2018). Any organisations need strong commitments to strive hard and meet their objectives. The same goes for Halal assets specificity, where service providers need to have high commitments in investing and providing the assets that meet the minimum requirements of the Halal compliance or standards. The responsibility will come together with commitments. Based on that, results that claimed Halal assets specificity and quality assurances are significant towards Halal Supply Chain Integrity were accepted without doubt. The results were also parallel with past works of literature that suggested both predictors as important factors towards the Halal Supply Chain Integrity (Awan et al., 2015; Othman et al., 2017; Susanty et al., 2020; Zulfakar et al., 2014).

The Relationship of Commitments as a Mediator Between Halal Traceability, Halal Assets Specificity, Halal Quality Assurance and Trust Towards Halal Supply Chain Integrity

The results indicated that the role of commitment was only significant between the relationship of trust and Halal Supply Chain Integrity compared to the other predictors' traceability, asset specificity and quality assurances. However, such a result did not conform with several past research that study the role of commitments mainly in the supply chain topic of study (Kim et al., 2020; Morgan et al., 2018; Shin et al., 2018; Stojanović & Ivetić, 2020; Wan Ahmad et al., 2016; Yuan et al., 2018; Živković et al., 2021).

One of the possible reasons is that commitment was mainly tested as a predictor towards Halal Supply Chain in the direct relationship rather than as a mediator between the predictors. Further investigations lead to a point where there could be a possible conflict between commitment and responsibility (Thomas, 2020). Commitment is defined as a promise or pledge to do something in the future (Friedman, 2022). At the same time, responsibility is more related to accountability (Thomas, 2020). Responsibility is the state or fact of having a duty to deal with something or of having control over someone. Both could be categorized as obligations but carry a different term and understanding (Liau, 2001). In general, responsibility refers to something for which one is responsible. The service providers are owed a job or duty to deal with it: they are accountable for the tasks especially related to the Halal integrity compliances.

Based on that, further research is needed to identify the use of commitments and responsibility in future research. Such things could be related to a specific term used in the questionnaires or even the definition of the term to be used in future studies.

The Direct Relationship of Commitments Towards Halal Supply Chain Integrity

A commitment was found to be significant in the relationship towards Halal Supply Chain Integrity. The higher the commitment, the higher the parties' willingness to commit to any specific matter. In order to establish and strengthen the commitment between parties in the supply chain, the respective parties must also show a certain level of commitment. The result parallels past research that indicated the significant relationship between commitment towards halal supply chain integrity. According to Lu et al. (2006), the level of commitment of the supply chain partners can be visibility seen when both firms are willing to increase their investment in the asset specificity to serve the special needs of their partners. In the context of the Halal food supply chain, commitments such as willingness to enhance the integrity of the Halal food supply chain (Aini & Safira, 2021; Sarbani & Suzana Jaafar, 2017; Zulfakar et al., 2014). By displaying a high level of commitment, all parties in the Halal supply chain can play shared roles in protecting and ensuring that Halal integrity will be at the highest level.

The Relationship of Barriers as a Moderator Between Commitments Towards Halal Supply Chain Integrity

The result indicated that barriers were insignificant as moderators between commitments and Halal Supply Chain Integrity. Such a result was interesting as it shows that responsibilities are very strong, which can turn the barriers ineffective. There are past studies in a different industry that claimed the same (Agyemang et al., 2018; Chowdhury et al., 2018; Hussain et al., 2019; Kaur et al., 2019; Moktadir et al., 2018; Siswanto et al., 2019; Vafadarnikjoo et al., 2021; Walker et al., 2008).

Based on the above, it can be concluded that high commitments are necessary to meet the objectives of Halal Supply Chain Integrity.

Part III

Conclusion, Contribution to the Supply Chain Literature and Proposed Future Research

Conclusion

To conclude, research in the area of halal supply chain is still lacking and findings from this chapter could further be enhanced. The next section will briefly explain how the study contributed to the knowledge.

Contributions of the Research

This present study contributes to the current literature by extending the understanding HSCI practices among LSP. Thus, the research helped address the gaps by developing an empirical model that examines the halal supply chain integrity among halal logistics service providers in Malaysia. These contributions and implications are discussed further below.

Theoretical Contribution

This research's contribution from the theoretical perspective lies in identifying halal traceability, assets specificity, quality assurance, trust, commitment and barriers in the halal supply chain integrity among the halal logistics service providers in Malaysia. This study contributes to the literature by investigating the main factor in determining halal supply chain integrity from the halal logistics service providers in Malaysia. The finding of this study contributes to the empirical knowledge towards determining halal supply chain integrity.

New kinds of literature in the field of Halal logistics and supply chain with extending halal integrity measurement items. As mentioned in the earlier chapters, most studies were conducted using qualitative research, and less research was found on quantitative. This research indirectly confirmed the proposed theoretical framework proposed by other past researchers through statistical evidence. At the same time this research indirectly opens more opportunities for future research

DOI: 10.4324/9781003305682-12

to explore the halal studies in a quantitative method. The use of mediators and moderators contributes to the knowledge of the current state of the relationship that other researchers can investigate further.

Apart from that, this research also introduced a set of questionnaires designed carefully under subject matter experts' supervision. Such questionnaires will be useful for future research in expanding their studies related to the halal supply chain. At the same time, there is a very high chance that this thesis will be used as the main reference by future researchers, thus contributing to more citations and references.

The study also validates the role of halal traceability, assets specificity, quality assurance, trust, commitment and barriers in the halal supply chain integrity among the halal logistics service providers in Malaysia. The findings also proved that asset specificity, quality assurance and trust are less critical in predicting halal supply chain integrity among HLSP. Therefore, this study provided insight into this issue and added to the body of knowledge in HSCI.

Methodological

This study eventually opened up more room for quantitative research concerning halal practices in Malaysia. Simultaneously, the study validated the previous research conducted by Ab Talib (2020), Noorliza (2020), Raut et al., (2019), Tieman and Ghazali (2014) and Zulfakar et al. (2014) with valid statistical evidence. Indirectly, the results of this study can be used by future studies to measure and explore additional variables and control variables that may deem suitable for further research. The framework used in this study can be adapted or adapted further to satisfy literature gaps related to the halal supply chain and other related halal integrity scopes of research.

However, this research provides a new halal studies platform related to halal logistics and halal supply chain, specifically Malaysia. Future studies can enhance the framework by testing new control variables that may deem suitable based on literature. There is a lack of empirical evidence in previous research on halal integrity items in quantitative study, thus this thesis can be the main source of references, in theory, methodology, and variables.

Practical Contribution

The contribution of this research lies in identifying how various factors impact HSCI. This study's contribution is to model all the relationships between HSCI and their determinants and simultaneously test these relationships. This work studied HSCI from the perspective of HLSP, which is less concerned by earlier researchers. Thus, this research fills in the last research gap. It was also essential to know that the difference in the industry contributed to a change of perception, collaboration, and paradigm shift among HLSP.

These studies can be useful for government agencies, especially those involved in the policymaking, enforcement and training in halal matters. The result showed the current state of response from the actual industry players in the market. As such, those results can be used for future strategic planning and troubleshooting of the current halal issues related to the halal supply chain in Malaysia.

Finally, the study also provides insightful information about the current behaviours of all the industry players in the halal logistics industry related to the halal industry. As such, the result should be useful for any halal industry stakeholders to look at the areas of improvement for future market expansion and enforcement. Relevant parties focus on the elements of Trust and commitments as well as barriers that contribute to integrity issues in the future.

Limitations

The study has several limitations when interpreting and generalizing the results as below. First, this research framework investigates four factors as predictors of HSCI among HLSP. Although those four were highly derived from the literature, future researchers may add more predictors that can be tested.

This study involved HLSP in Malaysia only. The result mainly focused on the specific industry. The research data were distributed and collected from 130 HLSP listed by JAKIM. However, the list of HLSP approved by JAKIM will be changed regularly annually based on the appointments and approval that are subject to compliances and audit reports. Getting responses and cooperation from all the HLSP are rather very tough. Many refuse and are reluctant to participate. Few attempts were made with the support from selected people who influence the HLSP to gain their support. A further empirical study in a bigger context may be performed quantitatively. Multiple case study approaches may also be adopted to get a more in-depth insight into understanding the determinant of HSCI from the HLSP perspective in Malaysia.

Appendix

Instructions to Respondents

This questionnaire consists of 7 sections, and you are requested to answer all the questions in all the sections. Your response in answering this questionnaire will be treated strictly confidential and will be used only for the purpose of this study. The information provided will not be forwarded or employed by any other individual or organization.

As a respondent you may perceive the question differently, there is no right or wrong answers. What is important is you have to answer all the questions as honest as you can by reading all the questions as carefully as you can.

Section 1: Company Profile

Please answer this section by ticking the box.

1 Company Name: ⎯⎯⎯⎯⎯⎯⎯⎯⎯⎯⎯⎯⎯⎯⎯⎯⎯
2 Company Address: ⎯⎯⎯⎯⎯⎯⎯⎯⎯⎯⎯⎯⎯⎯⎯
⎯⎯⎯⎯⎯⎯⎯⎯⎯⎯⎯⎯⎯⎯⎯⎯⎯⎯⎯⎯⎯⎯⎯⎯⎯⎯
⎯⎯⎯⎯⎯⎯⎯⎯⎯⎯⎯⎯⎯⎯⎯⎯⎯⎯⎯⎯⎯⎯⎯⎯⎯⎯
3 Contact Person: ⎯⎯⎯⎯⎯⎯⎯⎯⎯⎯⎯⎯⎯⎯⎯⎯
4 Position in the organization

	Owner
	Director
	Manager/assistant manager
	Senior executive officer/executive officer

5 Religion

	Muslim
	Non-Muslim

6 Gender

	Male
	Female

7 What is your age group?

21–35
36–50
51–65
Above 65

8 Educational qualifications
What is your age group?

	Post Graduate
	Graduate
	Diploma
	Post-Secondary

9 Working Experience – Managerial Level

	3 years or less
	4–10 years
	>10 years
	<20 years

10 Working Experience Sector

	Transportation/warehouse
	Logistics & supply chain
	Halal supply chain
	Others

11 Number of employees (approximately) in your organization:

	Less than 10
	11–200
	201–500
	500–1000
	More than 1000

12 Number of years that your organization has been operating?

Less than 5 years
5–15 years
16–24 years
More than 25 years

Section 2: Traceability

SD – Strongly Disagree   D – Disagree   N – Neither Agree or Disagree A – Agree

SA – Strongly Agree
Mark the most appropriate response

STATEMENTS	SD 1	D 2	N 3	A 4	SA 5

Information & Communication Technology (ICT)

1 Our organization believes that ICT is important for halal traceability

2 Our organization uses ICT to monitor real-time tracking

3 Our organization believes the usage of ICT will expedite the customs clearance process for HLSP

4 Our organization feels satisfied with the current halal traceability systems

5 Our organization needs to upgrade the current halal traceability systems for improvement

Logistics Control

6 Our organization believes effective halal traceability systems will improve service quality to customers

7 Our organization monitors shipment reach within scheduled time through traceability systems

8 Our organization has good logistics control on shipment movement

Innovative Capability

9 Our organization does inspire employees towards innovative ideas on halal traceability

10 Our organization does encourage employees towards innovative ideas to improve halal traceability

Section 3: Assets Specificity

SD – Strongly Disagree   D – Disagree   N – Neither Agree or Disagree

A – Agree SA – Strongly Agree
Mark the most appropriate response

Statements	SD 1	D 2	N 3	A 4	SA 5
Resource					
1 Our organization provides infrastructure for warehousing facilities in ensuring HSC integrity					
2 Our organization provides infrastructure for transport facilities in ensuring HSC integrity					
3 Our organization provides assets specificity as recommended by the halal authority					
4 Our organization has resources available to cater our customers' needs					
Physical Segregation					
5 Our organization ensures the appropriate transport for difference type of customers halal products					
6 Our organization provides dedicated warehouse for storage of our customers halal products					
7 Our organization ensures dedicated vehicles to transport our customers halal products					
Investment					
8 Our organization believes in the need for financial stability for asset specificity investment					
9 Our organization believes that investment in the asset specificity will be a return of investment (ROI)					
10 Our organization is willing to invest in asset specificity to cater our customers needs					

Section 4: Quality Assurance

SD – Strongly Disagree   D – Disagree   N – Neither Agree or Disagree

A – Agree SA – Strongly Agree
Mark the most appropriate response

Statements	SD 1	D 2	N 3	A 4	SA 5

Halal Policy

1 Our organization shared our halal policy to all employees to ensure quality assurance

2 Our organization follows halal policy for the quality assurance improvement

3 Our organization has competent internal halal committee to advise on halal policy

Halal Standard

4 Our organization has a written halal standard as guidelines to all employees

5 Our organization is aware of the Halal Standard MS2400 Halal Supply Chain

6 Our organization follows the halal standard and practices for quality assurance in ensuring HSC integrity

Halal Certification

7 Our organization understands the process of halal certification

8 Our organization has halal executive to handle our halal matters enquiries

9 Our organization has trained employees to manage our customers halal shipment

10 Our organization follows the guideline of halal certification for audit purposes

Section 5: Trust

SD – Strongly Disagree   D – Disagree   N – Neither Agree
                                                  or Disagree
A – Agree SA – Strongly Agree
Mark the most appropriate response

Items	*SD 1*	*D 2*	*N 3*	*A 4*	*SA 5*
Customers Relationship					
1 Our organization builds trust in customers relationship for business sustainability					
2 Our organization believes in the importance of trust in building customer relationships					
3 Our organization has customer loyalty programmes for long-term business collaboration					
Halal Risk Management					
4 Our organization believes that Halal Risk Management is important for HLSP					
5 Our organization follows the guidelines in the Halal Risk Management					
Company Policy					
6 Our organization's written company policy is a guideline for all employees					
7 Our organization believes that all employees must understand the company policy					
8 Our organization's company policy is trustworthy to all stakeholders					
9 Our organisation has an introductory of company policy to all new employees					

Section 6: Commitment

SD – Strongly Disagree   D – Disagree   N – Neither Agree or Disagree

A – Agree SA – Strongly Agree
Mark the most appropriate response

Items	*SD* *1*	*D 2*	*N 3*	*A 4*	*SA* *5*

Management Responsibility

1 Our organization is committed towards our customers' requirements
2 Our organization believes in the importance of commitment in customers' relationship
3 Our organization believes that all employees are committed to our customers' requirement
4 Our organization has developed customers loyalty programme
5 Our organization always gives quality service for customers retention

Halal Training

6 Our organization is committed to halal training for all employees
7 Our organization engages with halal local authority for training our employees
8 Our organization always trained our employees for customers satisfaction
9 Our organization has halal training programmes to ensure halal supply chain awareness
10 Our organization is reliable at all times in ensuring HSC integrity

Halal Personnel

11 Our organization has a dedicated internal halal committee
12 Our organization emphasizes on qualified halal personnel to handle customers halal shipment
13 Our organization encourages transparency in managing customers complaints
14 Our organization selected halal personnel who are qualified in Halal Supply Chain experience
15 Our organization emphasizes that halal personnel uphold halal integrity in handling customers halal shipment

Section 7: Halal Supply Chain Integrity

SD – Strongly Disagree   D – Disagree   N – Neither Agree or Disagree

A – Agree SA – Strongly Agree
Mark the most appropriate response

Items	*SD 1*	*D 2*	*N 3*	*A 4*	*SA 5*
HSC Management System					
1 Our organization believes that halal traceability is the determinant of HSC integrity for HLSP					
2 Our organization believes trust is the determinant of HSC integrity for HLSP					
Maintenance of Halal Supply Chain					
3 Our organization believes halal quality assurance is the determinant of HSC integrity for HLSP					
4 Our organization believes that assets specificity is the determinant of HSC integrity for HLSP					
Role of Government					
5 Our organization believes that the role of government is crucial in exploring innovative idea in the HSC					
6 Our organization believes the government-industry relationship will encourage strong bonding towards profitability					

References

Ab Rashid, N., & Bojei, J. (2019). The relationship between halal traceability system adoption and environmental factors on Halal food supply chain integrity in Malaysia. *Journal of Islamic Marketing*, 11(1), 117–142. https://doi.org/10.1108/JIMA-01-2018-0016

Ab Talib, M. S. (2020). Identifying halal logistics constraints in Brunei Darussalam. *Journal of Islamic Marketing*, 12(6), 1145–1158. https://doi.org/10.1108/JIMA-09-2019-0189

Ab Talib, M. S., Abdul Hamid, A. B., & Chin, T. A. (2016). Can halal certification influence logistics performance? *Journal of Islamic Marketing*, 7(4), 461–475. https://doi.org/10.1108/JIMA-02-2015-0015

Ab Talib, M. S., Pang, L. L., & Ngah, A. H. (2020). The role of government in promoting halal logistics: a systematic literature review. *Journal of Islamic Marketing*, 12(9), 1682–1708. https://doi.org/10.1108/JIMA-05-2020-0124

Abd Rahman, A., Singhry, H. B., Hanafiah, M. H., & Abdul, M. (2017). Influence of perceived benefits and traceability system on the readiness for halal assurance system implementation among food manufacturers. *Food Control*. https://doi.org/10.1016/j.foodcont.2016.10.058

Abdul, M. (2011). *Introduction to Entrepreneurship*. Oxford: Fajar. ISBN: 978–983–4701291

Abdul, M., Ismail, H. H., & Johari, J. (2009). Consumer decision making process in shopping for Halal food in Malaysia. *China-USA Business Review*, 8(9), 40–47.

Abdul Aziz, Y, & Nyen Vui, C (2012). The role of halal awareness and halal certification in influencing non-muslims' purchase intention. In Proceedings of the 3rd International Conference on Business and Economic Research (3rd ICBER 2012) (pp, 1819–1830), Indonesia.

Abdul Hafaz Ngah, Yuserrie Zainuddin, & Ramayah Thurasamy. (2014). Modelling of halal warehouse adoption using partial least squares (PLS). *International Journal of Contemporary Business Management*, 1(1), 71–86. eISSN: REQUEST PENDING © 2014 Universiti Selangor

Abdul Rahman, N. A. (2012). The Car manufacturer (CM) and third party logistics provider (TPLP) relationship in the outbound delivery channel: a qualitative study of the Malaysian automotive industry. PhD thesis, Brunel University library.

Abdul Rahman, N. A., Mohammad, M. F., Abdul Rahim, S., & Mohd Noh, H. (2018). Implementing air cargo Halal warehouse: insight from Malaysia. *Journal of Islamic Marketing*, 9(3), 462–483. https://doi.org/10.1108/JIMA-09-2016-0071

Abdul Rahman, R., Rezai, G., Mohamed, Z., Shamsudin, M. N., & Sharifuddin, J. (2013). Malaysia as global Halal hub: OIC food manufacturers' perspective. *Journal of International Food & Agribusiness Marketing*, 25(1), 154–166.

Abdul Talib, H. H., Mohd Ali, K. A. & Jamaludin, K. R. (2008). Quality assurance in Halal food manufacturing in Malaysia: A preliminary study, paper presented to International Conference on Mechanical and Manufacturing Engineering (ICME2008), Johor Bahru, Malaysia.

Abdul Talib, M. S. (2014). Halal logistics in Malaysia: A SWOT analysis. *Journal of Islamic Marketing*, 5(3), 322–343.

Abdul Talib, M. S., & Abdul Hamid, A. B. (2014). External factors evaluation of Malaysia Halal logistics industry, paper presented to International Conference on Innovation Driven Supply Chain 2014, 26–28 March 2014, AIMST University.

Abdul Talib, M. S., Abdul Hamid, A. B., & Chin, T. A. (2015). Conceptualising the implementation of halal food certification: An institutional theory perspective, paper presented to International Malaysia Halal Conference (IMHALAL) 2015, 1–2 April 2015.

Abdul Talib, M. S., Abdul Hamid, A. B., Zulfakar, M. H., & Jeeva, A. S. (2014). Halal logistics PEST analysis: The Malaysia perspectives. *Asian Social Science*, 10(14), 119–131.

Abdul Talib, M. S., & Johan, M. R. M. (2012). Issues in Halal packaging: A conceptual paper. *International Business and Management*, 5(2), 94–98.

Ahmad et al. (2014). Factors influencing readiness towards Halal logistics among food- based logistics players in Malaysia. *UMK Procedia*, 1(2014), 42–49.

Ahmad, N., & Shariff, S. M. (2016). Supply chain management: Sertu cleansing for halal logistics integrity. *Procedia Economics and Finance*, 37(16), 418–425. https://doi.org/10.1016/s2212-5671(16)30146-0

Ahmed, W. (2019). The role of consumer willingness to pay for Halal certification. 2010. *Journal of Islamic Marketing*, 10(4), 1230–1244. https://doi.org/10.1108/JIMA-09-2018-0155

Al-Ansi, A., Olya, H. G. T., & Han, H. (2019). Effect of general risk on trust, satisfaction, and recommendation intention for Halal food. *International Journal of Hospitality Management*, 83, 210–219. https://doi.org/10.1016/j.ijhm.2018.10.017

Alfalla-Luque, R., Marin-Garcia, J. A., & Medina-Lopez, C. (2015). An analysis of the direct and mediated effects of employee commitment and supply chain integration on organizational performance. *International Journal of Production Economics*, 162, 242–257.

Ali, A., Xiaoling, G., Sherwani, M., & Ali, A. (2018a). Antecedents of consumers' Halal brand purchase intention: an integrated approach. *Management Decision*, 56(4), 715–735. https://doi.org/10.1108/MD-11-2016-0785

Ali, A., Xiaoling, G., Sherwani, M., & Ali, A. (2018b). Antecedents of consumers' Halal brand purchase intention: an integrated approach. *Management Decision*, 56(4), 715–735. https://doi.org/10.1108/MD-11-2016-0785

Ali, M. H., & Suleiman, N. (2018). Eleven shades of food integrity: A Halal supply chain perspective. *Trends in Food Science and Technology*, 71(April 2017), 216–224. https://doi.org/10.1016/j.tifs.2017.11.016

Ali, M. H., Tan, H. T., & Ismail, D. M. (2017a). A supply chain integrity framework for halal food. *British Food Journal*, 119(1), 20–38. doi:10.1108/BFJ-07-2016-0345.

Ali, M. H., Zhan, Y., Alam, S. S., Tse, Y. K., & Tan, K. H. (2017). Food supply chain integrity: The need to go beyond certification. *Industrial Management and Data Systems*, 117(8), 1589–1611. https://doi.org/10.1108/IMDS-09-2016-0357

Ali, M. H., Tan, K., & Makhbul, Z. (2013). Mitigating halal food integrity risk through supply chain integration. The 14th Asia Pacific Industrial Engineering and Management Systems Conference (APIEMS 2013), Cebu, Philippines, 3rd -6th December, 2013.

Alias, M. N., Shamsudin, M. F., Majid, Z. A., Hakim, M. N. (2020). Technopreneurship and digital era in global regulation. In Providing Seminar, 1–9.

Alias, M. N., Majid, Z. A., Baharudin, K., Shamsudin, M. F. (2020). Attitude factors as a mediator between University roles and entrepreneurial intentions. *Journal of Critical Reviews,* 7(19), 1884–1893.

Ambali, A. R., & Bakar, A. N. (2013). Halāl food and products in Malaysia: People's awareness and policy implications. *Intellectual Discourse*, 21(1), 7.

Ambali, A. R., & Bakar, A. N. (2014). People's awareness on halal foods and products: Potential issues for policy-makers. *Procedia - Social and Behavioral Sciences*, 121, 3–25. https://doi.org/10.1016/j.sbspro.2014.01.1104

Arif, S., Bakar, N. A., & Sidek, S. (2019). Impediment factors to successful usage of online Halal certification. *Humanities and Social Sciences Reviews*, 7(2), 135–145. https://doi.org/10.18510/hssr.2019.7214

Aslan, I., & Aslan, H. (2016). Halal foods awareness and future challenges. *British Journal of Economics, Management & Trade*, 12(3), 1–20. https://doi.org/10.9734/bjemt/2016/23861

Azahari Jamaludin, Abd Razak Mohd Yusoff, Hamidon Katan, Jimisiah Jaafar, Mohd Fauzi Zainol Abidin, Mohd Hazli Mohd Rosli, Mohd Radzi Zainuddin, Rosnizza Ramlan, Salwah Che Mat & Zawiah Abdul Majid. (2013). *Technopreneurship*. Oxford: Fajar. ISBN: 978–983-4703530

Aziz, A.A. and Zailani, S. (2016), 'Halal Logistics: The Role of Ports, Issues and Challenges', in D.S. Mutum, M.M. Butt, and M. Rashid (eds), *Advances in Islamic Finance, Marketing, and Management*, Bingley: Emerald Group Publishing Limited, pp. 309–321. https://doi.org/10.1108/978-1-78635-899-820161015

Bahrudin, S. S. M. (2011). Tracking and tracing technology for halal product integrity over the supply chain. International Conference of Electrical Engineering and informatics, Bandung, Indonesia.

Boni, A., & Forleo, M. B. (2019). Italian Halal food market development: Drivers and obstacles from experts. *Opinions* 10(4), 1245–1271. https://doi.org/10.1108/JIMA-05-2018-0087

Bowersox, D. J., Closs, D. J., & Cooper M. B. (2010). *Supply chain logistics management,* 3rd ed. Singapore: McGraw Hill.

Che Man, Y., Bojei, J., Sazili, A.Q., & Abdullah, A. N. (2007). Malaysia halal hub opportunities. In 4th Asian Livestock & Feed Industry Conference.

Chin, W. W. (1998). The partial least squares approach to structural equation modeling. Modern methods for business research, 295(2), 295–336.

Coyle, J. J., Novack, R. A., Gibson, B. J., & Bardi, E. J. (2011). *Management of transportation,* 7th ed. Singapore: South-Western Cengage Learning.

Creswell, J. W. (2009). *Research design: Qualitative, quantitative and mixed methods approaches.* 3rd ed. Thousand Oaks, CA: Sage.

Daud, S., Din, R. C., Bakar, S., Kadir, M. R., & Sapuan, N. M. (2011). Implementation of MS1500: 2009: A gap analysis. *Communications of the IBIMA,* 2011, 1–11.

Department of Islamic Development Malaysia. (2005). *Manual procedure of halal certification.* Malaysia: Department of Islamic Development Malaysia.

Department of Standards Malaysia. (2010a). *MS 2400–1:2010 (P): Halalan-Toyyiban assurance pipeline Part 1: Management system requirements for transportation of goods and/or cargo chain services.* Malaysia: Department of Standards Malaysia.

Department of Standards Malaysia. (2010b). *MS 2400–2:2010 (P): Halalan-Toyyiban assurance pipeline Part 2: Management system requirements warehouse and related activities.* Malaysia: Department of Standards Malaysia.

Department of Standards Malaysia. (2010c). *MS 2400–3:2010 (P): Halalan-Toyyiban assurance pipeline Part 3: Management system requirements for retailing.* Malaysia: Department of Standards Malaysia.

Department of Standards Malaysia. (2009). *MS1500:2009. Halal food – production, preparation, handling and storage – general guidelines.* 2nd ed. Malaysia: SIRIM QAS International.

Department of Standards Malaysia. (2010). *MS2400–1:2010. Halalan-toyyiban assurance pipeline – part 1: management system requirements for transportation of goods and/or cargo chain services.* Malaysia: Department of Standards Malaysia.

Department of Statistics Malaysia. (2020). *Malaysia economic performance fourth quarter 2019.* Mohd Uzir Mahidin. Prime Minister's Department, Department Of Statistics Malaysia.

Dubai International Financial Centre. (2019). *State of global islamic economy 2018.* Global Islamic Economy. https://ded.ae/DED_Files/Studies AndResearch/SGIE-Report-2018-19_Eng_1540649428.pdf

Dupuy, C., Botta-Genoulaz, V., & Guinet, A. (2005). Batch dispersion model to optimize traceability in food industry. *Journal of Food Engineering,* 70(3), 333–339.

European Commission. (2002). Regulation (EC) No 178/2002 of the European Parliament and of the Council. *Official Journal of the European Communities*, 31(1), 1–24.

Fathi, E., Zailani, S., Iranmanesh, M., & Kanapathy, K. (2016). Drivers of consumers' willingness to pay for Halal logistics. *British Food Journal*, 118(2), 464–479. https://doi.org/10.1108/BFJ

Fotopoulos, C., Kafetzopoulos, D. & Gotzamani, K. (2011). Critical factors for effective implementation of the HACCP system: a pareto analysis. *British Food Journal*, 113(5), 578–597.

Ghadikolaei, F. S. (2016). The effect of Halal signs and symptoms and consumers' purchase intention in Muslim and Non-Muslim countries: A review. *International Journal of Business and Management Invention*, 5(7), 44–49.

Gubbins, E. J. (2003). *Managing transport operation*. 3rd ed. Cornwall: Kogan Page.

Iberahim, H., Kamaruddin, R., & Shabudin, A. (2012, September). Halal development system: The institutional framework, issues and challenges for halal logistics. *In 2012 IEEE Symposium on Business, Engineering and Industrial Applications* (pp. 760–765). IEEE.

Hair, J., Anderson, R., Tatham, R., & Black, W. (1995). *Multivariate data analysis with readings*. 4th ed. Englewood Cliffs: Prentice-Hall International.

Hair, Jr., J. F., Hult, G. T. M., Ringle, C. M., & Sarstedt, M. (2017). *A primer on partial least squares structural equation modeling*. 2nd ed. Thousand Oaks, CA: SAGE Publication Inc.

Hair, Jr., J. F., Sarstedt, M., Hopkins, L., & Kuppelwieser, V. G. (2014). Partial least squares structural equation modeling (PLS-SEM): An emerging tool in business research. *European Business Review*, 26(2), 106–121.

Halal Development Corporation. (2012). Business opportunities in halal industry. MIHAS 2012 Halal Development Corporation (HDC) (20 May 2013). Retrieve from http://www.hdcglobal.com/publisher/alias/bu_Halal-directory?

Haleem, A., & Khan, M. I. (2017). Towards successful adoption of halal logistics and its' implications for the stakeholders. *British Food Journal*, 119, 7. doi:10.1108/ BFJ-12-2016-0637.

Haleem, A., Khan, M. I., & Khan, S. (2019). Halal certification, the inadequacy of its adoption, modelling and strategizing the efforts. *Journal of Islamic Marketing*, 11(2), 384–404. https://doi.org/10.1108/JIMA-05-2017-0062

Haleem, A., Khan, M. I., & Khan, S. (2020). Conceptualizing a framework linking Halal supply chain management with sustainability: An India centric study. *Journal of Islamic Marketing*, 12(8), 1535–1552. https://doi.org/10.1108/JIMA-07-2019-0149

Hamdan, J., & Sarbani, N. (2018). Enhancing halal logistics through trade facilitation. 5(4), 128–134. ISSN: 2348-4969 www.kaavpublications.org

Hammant, J. (1995). Information technology trends in logistics. *Logistics Information Management*, 8(6), 32–37.

Hanifah, M. F. H., Rafeah, S., Zakiah, S., Zulaipa, R., & Munirah, A. (2017). Social sciences & humanities maslahah approach in halal-logistics operation. *Pertanika Journal of Social Science & Humanities*, 2017, 25.

Harlina Suzana Jaafar, Intan Rohani Endut, Nasruddin Faisol, & Emi N. Omar. (2011). Innovation in logistics services: Halal logistics. Proceedings of the 16th International Symposium on Logistics (ISL), Berlin, Germany, 10–13 july, pp 844–851. ISBN: 978–085358-279-3.

Haroon Latif, M. T. A. (2016). What exactly does Halal certification involve and is it worth it? SalaamGateway.Com. https://salaamgateway.com/story/what-exactly-does-halal-certification-involve-and-is-it-worth-it

Hassan, M. H., Arif, S., & Sidek, S. (2015). Knowledge and practice for implementing internal Halal assurance system among Halal executives. *Asian Social Science*, 11(17), 57. https://doi.org/10.5539/ass.v11n17p57

Iberahim, H., Kamaruddin, R., & Shabudin, A. (2012). Halal development system: The institutional framework, issues and challenges for Halal logistics, paper presented at 2012 IEEE Symposium on Business, Engineering and Industrial Applications (ISBEIA), pp. 760–765.

Ik-Whan, G.K., & Taewon, S. (2005). Trust, commitment and relationships in supply chain management: A path analysis. *Supply Chain Management: An International Journal*, 10(1), pp. 26–33.

Indarti, N., Lukito-Budi, A. S., & Islam, A. M. (2020). A systematic review of Halal supply chain research: To where shall we go? *Journal of Islamic Marketing*, 12(9), 1930–1949. https://doi.org/10.1108/JIMA-05–2020–0161

Jaafar, H.S., Endut, I.R., Faisol, N., & Omar, E.N. (2011). Innovation in logistics services: Halal logistics, paper presented to 16th International Symposium on Logistics (ISL), Berlin, Germany, 10-13 July.

Jakim. (2013). Halal assurance system (Online) May 14. Available: http://www.Halal.gov.my/v3/index.php/ms/garis-panduan/sistem-jaminan-Halal/ (Accessed 16 October 2014).

Kamaruddin, R., Iberahim, H., & Shabudin, A. (2012). Willingness to pay for halal logistics. *The Lifestyle Choice*. 50(July), 722–729. https://doi.org/10.1016/j.sbspro.2012.08.075

Karia, N. (2019). Halal logistics: practices, integration and performance of logistics service providers. *Journal of Islamic Marketing*, 13(1), 100–118. https://doi.org/10.1108/JIMA-08-2018-0132

Khan, M. I., & Haleem, A. (2016). Understanding "Halal" and "Halal Certification & Accreditation System"- A brief review. *Saudi Journal of Business and Management Studies,* 1(1), 32–42.

Khan, M. I., Haleem, A., & Khan, S. (2018). Defining halal supply chain management. *Supply Chain Forum*, 19(2), 122–131. https://doi.org/10.1080/16258312.2018.1476776

Khan, S., Haleem, A., Khan, M., Abidi, M., & Al-Ahmari, A. (2018). Implementing traceability systems in specific supply chain management (scm) through critical success factors (Csfs). *Sustainability*, 10(2), 204. doi:10.3390/su10010204.

Kottala, S. Y., & Herbert, K. (2019). An empirical investigation of supply chain operations reference model practices and supply chain performance: Evidence from manufacturing sector. *International Journal of Productivity and Performance Management*, 69(9), 1925–1954. https://doi.org/10.1108/IJPPM-09-2018-0337

Krishnan, S., Omar, C. M. C., Zahran, I., Syazwan, N., & Alyaa, S. (2017). The awareness of gen z's toward halal food industry. *Management*, 7(1), 44–47.

Kwag, S. I., & Ko, Y. D. (2019). Optimal design for the Halal food logistics network. *Transportation Research Part E: Logistics and Transportation Review*, 128(June), 212–228. https://doi.org/10.1016/j.tre.2019.06.005

Lai, P. L., Su, D. T., Tai, H. H., & Yang, C. C. (2020). The impact of collaborative decision-making on logistics service performance for container shipping services. *Maritime Business Review*, 5(2), 175–191. https://doi.org/10.1108/MABR-12-2019-0061

Laldin, Mohamad Akram. (2006). *Islamic law – An introduction*. Malaysia: International Islamic University Malaysia.

Lancioni, R. A., Smith, M. F., & Oliva, T. A. (2000). The role of the internet in supply chain management. *Industrial Marketing Management*, 29, 45–56.

Lewis, I., & Talalayevsky, A. (2004). Improving the interorganizational supply chain through optimization of information flows. *Journal of Enterprise Information Management*, 17(3), 229–237. https://doi.org/10.1108/17410390410531470

Lu, H., Trienekens, J. H., & Omta, S. W. F. (2006). Does guanxi matter for vegetable supply chains in China? A case study approach. in J Bijman, SWF Omta, JH Trienekens, JHM Wijnands & EFM Wubben (eds), *International agri-food chains and networks: management and organization*. Wageningen: Wageningen Academic Publishers pp. 31–47.

Hijrah, M. A., Kadir, R., Zuraidah, R. M., & Sarah, S. (2016). Halal supply chain management streamlined practices: issues and challenges. In *IOP Conference Series: Materials Science and Engineering*. IOP Publishing, Vol. 160, No. 1, p. 012070.

Madhuri et al. (2014). Remote vehicle tracking and driver health monitoring system using GSM modem and google maps. *International Journal of Computer Science and Information Technology*, 5(3), 28282832.

Magnus Berglund, Peter van Laarhoven, Graham Sharman, & Sten Wandel. (1999). Third-party logistics: Is there a future? *The International Journal of Logistics Management*, 10(1), 59–70. http://dx.doi.org/10.1108/09574099910805932

Mahidin, N., Mustafar, M., Elias, E. M., & Abu Bakar, S. Z. (2019). Applying the theory of the planned behavior on Halal logistics services adoption among food & beverages small and medium enterprises. *International Journal of Supply Chain Management*, 8(4), 1039–1046.

Majid Z. A. et al. (2019). Halal Integrity from logistics service provider perspective. *International Journal of Supply Chain Management*, 8(5), October 2019.

Majid, Z. A., & Nitty Hirawaty Kamarulzaman. (2014). Developing halal food supply chain integrity model in logistics industry (a conceptual framework review), Malaysia International Halal Research & Education Conference (Marriot Hotel, Putrajaya Malaysia) Proceeding of Malaysia International Halal Research & Education Conference 2014, December 2–4.

Majid, Z. A., Nitty Hirawaty Kamarulzaman, & Nor Aida Abdul Rahman. (2015). Halal food supply chain: Logistics service providers (LSP) roles and challenges. Proceeding of LPPH-UKM Seminar on Shariah and Halal Laws, UPM 19 March 2015 ISBN 978-967-12398-1-0.

Majid, Z. A., Nitty Hirawaty Kamarulzaman, & Ruhaida Abdul Rashid, (2014), Developing halal food supply chain integrity model in logistics industry (research proposal review). Proceeding: The Chartered Institute Of Logistics and Transport, International Academic Conference on Logistics & Transport 2014 June, Melaka, Malaysia. ISBN: 978-967-12715-0-6.

Majid, Z. A., & Shamsudin, M. F. (2019). Advances in transportation and logistics. innovation in logistics from 1PL toward 10PL: Counting the numbers. *Research*, 2, 440–447.

Rahman, N. A. A., Majid, Z. A., Mohammad, M. F., Ahmad, M. F., Rahim, S. A., & Mokhtar, A. Z. (2020). The development of Halal logistics standards in South-East Asia: Halal supply chain standards (MS2400) as a principal reference. In Halal Logistics and Supply Chain Management in Southeast Asia (pp. 149–160). Routledge.

Mayer, R. C., Davis, J., & Schoorman, F. D. (1995). An integrative model of organizational trust. *Academy of Management Review*, 20(3), 709–34.

Meuwissen, M. P., Velthuis, A. G., Hogeveen, H., & Huirne, R. B. (2003). Traceability and certification in meat supply chains. *Journal of Agribusiness*, 21(2), 167–182.

Ministry of International Trade and Industry Malaysia (MITI). (2006). *Malaysia third industrial plan (IMP3) 2006–2020*. Kuala Lumpur: Pencetakan Nasional Malaysia Berhad.

Moe, T. (1998). Perspectives on traceability in food manufacture. *Trends in Food Science & Technology*, 9(5), 211–214.

Mohamed, M. I. K. P. H. P., Yusoff, W. F. W., & Rasi, R. Z. R. M. (2018). Bumiputra SMES food manufactures halal certification challenges: A review. *Advanced Science Letters*, 24(5), 3234–3239. https://doi.org/10.1166/asl.2018.11349

Mohamed Syazwan Ab Talib, Abu Bakar, & Mohd Hafiz Zulfakar. (2013). Halal supply chain critical success factors: A literature review. *Journal of Islamic Marketing*, 6(1), 44–71. http://dx.doi.org/10.1108/JIMA-07-2013-0049

Mohamed Syazwan Ab Talib, Abu Bakar, Mohd Hafiz Zulfakar, & Thoo Ai Chin. (2015). Barriers to halal logistics operation: Views from Malaysian logistics experts. *International Journal of Logistics Systems and Management*. 22(22), 193–209. DOI:10.1504/IJLSM.2015.071545

Mohamed Syazwan Ab Talib, Lim Rubin, & Vincent Khor Zhenyi. (2013). Qualitative research on critical issues in halal logistics. *Journal of Emerging Economies and Islamic Research*, 1(2), 1–20.

Mohamed, Y. H., Abdul Rahim, A. R., & Ma'aram, A. (2020). The effect of Halal supply chain management on Halal integrity assurance for the food industry in Malaysia. *Journal of Islamic Marketing*, 12(9), 1734–1750. https://doi.org/10.1108/JIMA-12-2018-0240

Mohammad Fakhrulnizam, M., Nor Aida, A. R., Ahmad, Z., & Zawiah, A. M. (2014). A literature review and future agenda of Halal Logistics study, Malaysia International Halal Research & Education Conference (Marriot Hotel, Putrajaya Malaysia) Proceeding of Malaysia International Halal Research & Education Conference 2014, December 2–4.

Mohammed Laeequddin, B. S., Sahay Vinita Sahay, K., & Abdul Waheed. (2010). Measuring trust in supply chain partners' relationships. *Measuring Business Excellence*, 14(3), 53–69.

Mohd Helmi Ali, Kim Hua Tan, & Md Daud Ismail. (2017). A supply chain integrity framework for Halal food. *British Food Journal*, 119(1), 20–38. https://doi.org/10.1108/BFJ-07-2016-0345.

Mohd Imran Khan, & Abid Haleem. (2016). Understanding "Halal" and "Halal Certification & Accreditation System" - A brief review. *Saudi Journal of Business and Management Studies*, 1(1), 32–42.

Mohd Imran Khan, Abid Haleem, & Shahbaz Khan. (2018). Defining halal supply chain management, supply chain forum. *An International Journal*, 19(2), 122–131. DOI: 10.1080/16258312.2018.1476776

Mohd Iskandar Illyas Tan. (2012). Factors influencing ict adoption in halal transportations: A case study of malaysian halal logistics service providers. *IJCSI International Journal of Computer Science Issues*, 9(1), 1694.

Mohd Nasir Alias, Zawiah Abd Majid, Baharudin Kadir, Siti Aisyah Esa, & Mohd Farid Shamsudin. (2020). Relationship of attitude factors towards students entrepreneurial intentions. *Journal of Critical Reviews*, 7(19), 1902–1908. doi:10.31838/jcr.07.19.231

Muhammad, A., Ab Talib, M. S., Hussein, M. Z. S. M., & Jaafar, H. S. (2018). Motivations to implement halal logistics management standards: A review. In Proceedings of the 3rd International Halal Conference (INHAC 2016). https://doi.org/10.1007/978-981-10-7257-4_30

Muhammad, N. M. N., Isa, F. M., & Kifli, B. C. (2009). Positioning Malaysia as halal hub: Integration role of supply chain strategy and halal assurance system. *Asian Social Science*, 5(7), 44–52.

Murphy, P. R., & Wood, D. F. (2004). *Contemporary logistics*. 8th ed. Singapore: Pearson Prentice Hall.

Ngah, A. H., Thurasamy, R., Aziz, N. A., Ali, M. H., & Khan, M. I. (2019). Modelling the adoption of Halal warehousing services among Halal pharmaceutical and cosmetic manufacturers. *Journal of Sustainability Science and Management*, 14(6), 103–116.

Ngah, A. H., Zainuddin, Y., & Thurasamy, R. (2014). Adoption of halal supply chain among malaysian halal manufacturers: An exploratory study. *Procedia - Social and Behavioral Sciences*, 129, 388–395. https://doi.org/10.1016/j.sbspro.2014.03.692

Nik Maheran, Nik Muhammad, Filzah Md Isa, & Bidin Chee Kifli. (2009). Positioning Malaysia as halal-hub:integration role of supply chain strategy and halal assurance system. *Asian Social Science,* 5(7), 44–52.

Noordin, N., Md Noor, N. L., & Samicho, Z. (2014). Strategic approach to Halal certification system: an ecosystem perspective. *Procedia – Social and Behavioral Sciences,* 121, 79–95.

Noorliza, K. (2020). Resource-capability of Halal logistics services, its extent and impact on performance. *Journal of Islamic Marketing,* 12(4), 813–829. https://doi.org/10.1108/JIMA-12-2019-0255

Nor, M. R. M., Latif, K., & Ismail, M. N. (2016). Critical success factors of halal supply chain management from the perspective of Malaysian halal food manufacturers. *Nigerian Chapter of Arabian Journal of Business and Management Review,* 4(1), 1–23. https://doi.org/10.12816/0031515

Norman, A. A., Nasir, M. H. N. M., Fauzi, S. S. M., & Azmi, M. (2009). Consumer acceptance of rfid- enabled services in validating halal status. 9th International Symposium on Communications and Information Technology, ISCIT 2009, 911–915.

Novais, L., Maqueira Marín, J. M., & Moyano-Fuentes, J. (2020). Lean production implementation, cloud-supported logistics and supply chain integration: Interrelationships and effects on business performance. *International Journal of Logistics Management,* 31(3), 629–663. https://doi.org/10.1108/IJLM-02-2019-0052

Omar, E. N., & Jaafar, H. S. (2011). Halal supply chain in the food industry: A conceptual model, paper presented to 2011 IEEE Symposium on Business, Engineering and Industrial Applications (ISBEIA), 25–28 September. 2011.

Omar, E. N., Jaafar, H. S., & Osman, M. R. (2013). Halalan toyyiban supply chain of the food industry. *Journal of Emerging Economies and Islamic Research,* 1, 1–12.

Omar, E. N., & Jaafar H. S., & Rahimi M. (2014). Halalan toyyiban supply chain the new insights in sustainable supply chain management, (2013): 137. online at http://mpra.ub.uni- muenchen.de/52756/MPRA Paper No. 52756, posted 10. January 2014 09.50UTC

Othman, B., Shaarani, S. M., & Bahron, A. (2016a). Social sciences & humanities, the potential of asean in halal certification implementation: A review. *Pertanika Journal of Social Science and Humanities,* 24(1), 1–24.

Othman, B., Shaarani, S. M., & Bahron, A. (2016b). The potential of ASEAN in Halal certification implementation: A review. *Pertanika Journal of Social Sciences and Humanities,* 24(1), 1–24.

Othman, P., Sungkar, I., & Hussin, W. S. W. (2009). Malaysia as an international halal food hub competitiveness and potential of meat-based industries. *ASEAN Economic Bulletin,* 26(3), 306–320.

Pahim, K. M., Jemali, S., Jamal, S., Nasir, A., & Mohamad, S. (2012). The importance of training for Halal logistics industry in Malaysia, Humanities. In *Science and Engineering Research (SHUSER).* IEEE Symposium on Halal Logisctics, Kuala Lumpur.

Pahim, K. M. B., Jemali, S., & Mohamad, S. J. A. N. S. (2012a). An empirical research on relationship between demand, people and awareness towards training needs: A case study in Malaysia Halal logistics industry, paper presented to Business Engineering and Industrial Applications Colloquium (BEIAC), 2012 IEEE, 7–8 April 2012.

Pahim, K. M. B., Jemali, S., & Mohamad, S. J. A. N. S. (2012b). The importance of training for Halal logistics industry in Malaysia, paper presented to Humanities, Science and Engineering Research (SHUSER), 2012 IEEE Symposium on, 24–27 June 2012.

Peters, B. G. (2016). Institutional theory. In *Handbook on Theories of Governance*. Edward Elgar Publishing, pp. 323–335. https://doi.org/10.1093/acprof:oso/9780199296576.003.0002

Poniman, D., Purchase, S., & Sneddon, J. (2014). Traceability systems in the Western Australia. *Halal Food Supply Chain*, 27(2), 324–348. https://doi.org/10.1108/APJML-05-2014-0082

Price Waterhouse Coopers. (2008). *From vulnerable to valuable: how integrity can transform a supply chain*. Achieving operational excellence series

Pun, K. F., & Bhairo-Beekhoo, P. (2008). Factors affecting HACCP practices in the food sectors: A review of literature 1994–2007. *Asian Journal on Quality*, 9(1), 134–152.

Quoquab, F., Mohamed Sadom, N. Z., & Mohammad, J. (2019). Driving customer loyalty in the Malaysian fast food industry: The role of Halal logo, trust and perceived reputation. *Journal of Islamic Marketing*, 11(6), 1367–1387. https://doi.org/10.1108/JIMA-01-2019-0010

Rahman, N. A. A., Majid, Z. A., & Mohammad, M. F. (2020). Institutional theory: A general review. *Journal of Advanced Research in Dynamical & Control Systems*, 12(06), 2020.

Rahman, N. A. A., Majid, Z. A., Mohammad, M. F. N., Ahmad, M. F., Rahim, S. F. (2020). The development of Halal Logistics standards in South-East Asia: Halal supply chain standards (MS2400) as a principal reference. *Halal Logistics and Supply Chain Management in Southeast Asia*. Routledge, pp. 149–160.

Rahman, N. A. A., Mohammad, M. F., Muda, J., Noh, H. M., Majid, Z. A., Rahim, Z. A. (2018). Linking halal requirement and branding: An examination of halal flight kitchen provider in Malaysia. *International Journal of Supply Chain Management*, 7(3), 208–215.

Raut, R. D., Gardas, B. B., Narwane, V. S., & Narkhede, B. E. (2019). Improvement in the food losses in fruits and vegetable supply chain: A perspective of cold third-party logistics approach. *Operations Research Perspectives*, 6(June), 100117. https://doi.org/10.1016/j.orp.2019.100117

Rejeb et al. (2018). Halal meat supply chain traceability based on HACCP, block chain and internet of things. *Acta Technica Jaurinensis*, 11(1).

Riaz, M. N., & Chaundry, M. M. (2004). *Halal food production*. CRC Press. Richardson.

Roth, A. V., Tsay, A. A., Pullman, M. E., & Gray, J. V. (2008). Unraveling the food supply chain: strategic insights from China and the 2007 recalls. *Journal of Supply Chain Management*, 44(1), 22–39.

Rowley, J. (2014). Designing and using research questionnaires. *Management Research Review*, 37(3), 308–330. https://doi.org/10.1108/MRR-02-2013-0027

Saidi, S., & Hammami, S. (2011). The role of transport and logistics to attract foreign direct investment in the developing countries. 4th International Conference on Logistics (LOGISTIQUA 2011) (pp. 484–489). Hammamet, Tunisia: IEEE.

Samori, Z., Ishak, A. H., & Kassan, N. H. (2014). Understanding the development of halal food standard: suggestion for future research. *International Journal of Social Science and Humanity*, 4(6), 482–486. https://doi.org/10.7763/IJSSH.2014.V4.403

Scott, W. R. (1987). The adolescence of institutional theory. *Administrative Science Quarterly*. https://doi.org/10.2307/2392880

Sekaran, U., & Bougie, R. (2009). *Research method for business: A skill building approach*. Singapore: Wiley.

Selim, N. I. I. B., Zailani, S., Aziz, A. A., & Rahman, M. K. (2019). Halal logistic services, trust and satisfaction amongst Malaysian 3PL service providers. *Journal of Islamic Marketing*, 13(1), 81–99. https://doi.org/10.1108/JIMA-05-2018-0088

Shafie, S., & Othman, M. N. (2004). Halal certification: an international marketing issues and challenges. In Proceeding at the International IFSAM VIIIth World Congress. Kuala Lumpur: University of Malaya Press, Vol. 28, p. 30.

Shahid, S., Ahmed, F., & Hasan, U. (2018). A qualitative investigation into consumption of Halal cosmetic products: The evidence from India. *Journal of Islamic* Marketing, 9(3), 484–503. https://doi.org/10.1108/JIMA-01-2017-0009

Sham, R., Rasi, R. Z., Abdamia, N., Mohamed, S., & Thahira Bibi, T. K. M. (2017). Halal logistics implementation in Malaysia: a practical view. In IOP Conference Series: Materials Science and Engineering. IOP Publishing, Vol. 226, No. 1, p. 012040. https://doi.org/10.1088/1757-899X/226/1/012040

Shamsudin, M. F. (2015). Determinants of customer loyalty in the telecommunications industry: A study of prepaid mobile segment in Malaysia, Doctorate Thesis UUM.

Shamsudin, M. F., Hassan, S., Majid, Z. A., & Ishak, M. F. (2020). How halal brand trust and halal brand image influence halal brand purchasing intention. *Journal of Critical Reviews*, 7(4), 1097–1103.

Sheppard, B., & Sherman, D. (1998). 'The grammars of trust: a model and general implications. *Academy of Management Review*, 23(3), 422–437.

Sherwani, M., Ali, A., Ali, A., & Hussain, S. (2018). Determinants of Halal meat consumption in Germany. *Journal of Islamic Marketing*, 9(4), 863–883. https://doi.org/10.1108/JIMA-01-2018-0009.

Soon, J. M., Chandia, M., & Regenstein, J. M. (2017). Halal integrity in the food supply chain. *British Food Journal,* 119(1), 39–51. doi:10.1108/BFJ-04-2016-0150.

Soon, J. M., & Wallace, C. (2017). Application of theory of planned behaviour in purchasing intention and consumption of Halal food. *Nutrition and Food Science*, 47(5), 635–664. https://doi.org/10.1108/NFS-03-2017-0059

Soong, V. (2007). Managing Halal quality in food service industry, Professional paper thesis, University of Nevada, Las Vegas, NV.

Soraji, A. J., Awang, M. D., & Mohd Yusoff, A. N. (2017). Malaysia halal trust: Between reality and challenges. *Ijasos- International E-Journal of Advances in Social Sciences*, 3(7), 197–204. https://doi.org/10.18769/ijasos.309676

Suhaiza, H. M. Z., Zainal, A. A., Nabsiah, A. W., Rosly, Y. F. (2010). Recommendations to strengthen halal food supply chain for food industry in Malaysia. *Journal of Agribusiness Marketing*, 2010, 91–105.

Susanty, A., Puspitasari, N. B., Caterina, A. D., & Jati, S. (2020). Mapping the barriers for implementing Halal logistics in Indonesian food, beverage and ingredient companies. *Journal of Islamic Marketing*, 12(4), 649–669. Https://doi.org/10.1108/JIMA-11-2019-0244

Synodinos, N. E. (2003). The "art" of questionnaire construction: Some important considerations for manufacturing studies. *Integrated Manufacturing Systems*, 14(3), 221–237. https://doi.org/10.1108/09576060310463172

Talib, A., Ali, M., Anuar, K., & Jamaludin, K. R. (2008). Quality assurance in Halal food manufacturing in Malaysia: A preliminary study, paper presented to International Conference on Mechanical & Manufacturing Engineering (ICME2008), 21–23 May 2008, Johor Bahru.

Talib, Z., Zailani, S., & Zainuddin, Y. (2010). Conceptualizations on the dimensions for the Halal orientation for food manufacturers: A study in the context of Malaysia. *Pakistan Journal of Social Sciences*, 7(2), 56–61.

Tan, K. H., Ali, M. H., Makhbul, Z. M., & Ismail, A. (2017). The impact of external integration on halal food integrity. *Supply Chain Management: An International Journal*, 22(2), 186–199. https://doi.org/10.1108/SCM-05-2016-0171

Tan, M. I., Razali, R. N., & Husny, Z. J. (2012). Factors influencing ICT adoption in Halal transportation: A case study of Malaysian Halal logistics service providers. *International Journal of Computer Science Issues*, 9(1), 62–71.

Tarmizi, H. A., Kamarulzaman, N. H., Latiff, I. A., & Rahman, A. A. (2014). Factors influencing readiness towards halal logistics among food-based logistics players in Malaysia. *UMK Procedia*, 1(October 2013), 42–49. https://doi.org/10.1016/j.umkpro.2014.07.006

Tieman, M. (2011). The application of Halal in supply chain management: In-depth interviews. *Journal of Islamic Marketing*, 2(2), 186–195. https://doi.org/10.1108/17590831111139893

Tieman, M. (2013). The application of halal in supply chain management: principles in the design and management of halal food supply chain, PhD Thesis, Universiti Teknologi Mara.

Tieman, M., & Ghazali, A. P. D. M. C. (2012). Halal control activities and assurance activities in Halal food logistics, paper presented to International Halal Conference 2012 (INHAC), Kuala Lumpur, Malaysia, 4–5 September 2012.

Tieman, M., & Ghazali, M. C. (2014). Halal control activities and assurance activities in Halal food logistics. *Procedia-Social and Behavioral Sciences*, 121, 44–57.

Tieman, M., Van de Vorst, J. G., & Ghazali, M. C. (2012). Principles in Halal supply chain management. *Journal of Islamic Marketing*, 3(3), 217–243.

Tseng, Y. Y., Yue, W. L., & Taylor, M. A. (2005). The role of transportation in logistics chain. *Proceedings of the Eastern Asia Society for Transportation Studies*, 5(135), 1655–1672.

Urbach, N., & Ahlemann, F. (2010). Structural equation modeling in information systems research using partial least squares. Journal of Information Technology Theory and Application (JITTA), 11(2), 2.

Vanany, I., Maarif, G. A., & Soon, J. M. (2019). Application of multi-based quality function deployment (QFD) model to improve Halal meat industry. *Journal of Islamic Marketing*, 10(1), 97–124. https://doi.org/10.1108/JIMA-10-2017-0119

Vanany, I., Soon, J. M., Maryani, A., & Wibawa, B. M. (2019). Determinants of Halal-food consumption in Indonesia. *Journal of Islamic Marketing*, 11(2), 507–521. https://doi.org/10.1108/JIMA-09-2018-0177

Vlajic, J. V., Vorst, J. G. A. J., & van der Haijema, R. (2012). A framework for designing robust food supply chains. *International Journal of Production Economics*, 137, 176–189.

Wan Hassan, W. M. (2008). *Halal restaurants in New Zealand: Implications for the hospitality and tourism industry*. Doctoral dissertation, University of Otago. New Zealand: University of Otago.

Wan Ismail, W. R., Othman, M., Md Nor, N., Badiuzaman, A. F., & Nik Mohd Nor, N. M. S. (2020). Halal Malaysia brand equity mishap: False recognition of brand mere recognition using mixed method approach. *Journal of Islamic Marketing*. https://doi.org/10.1108/JIMA-04-2019–0073

Wan Omar, M. (2014). Developing a model for halal food supply chain implementation, PhD Thesis, RMIT University.

Werts, C. E., Linn, R. L., & Jöreskog, K. G. (1974). Intraclass reliability estimates: Testing structural assumptions. Educational and Psychological measurement, 34(1), 25–33.

Wilson, J. A., & Liu, J. (2010). Shaping the Halal into a brand?. *Journal of Islamic Marketing*, 1(2), 107–123.

Wong, K. K.-K. (2013). Partial least squares structural equation modeling (PLS-SEM) techniques using SmartPLS. *Marketing Bulletin*, 24(1), 1–32.

World Population Review. (2020). *Countries by density 2020*. World Population Review. https://worldpopulationreview.com/country-rankings/countries-by-density

Yahaya, M. L., Oyediran, O. S., & Onukuwbe, H. N. (2019). Evaluating Factors Affecting Transaction Costs of Contractors in Public Procurement in Nigeria: PLS-SEM Approach. *FUTY Journal of the Environment*, 13(1), 46–64.

Yasin, K. (2011). UIAM, JAKIM usaha tingkat industri Halal. Available: http://www.bharian.com.my/bharian/articles/UIAM_JAKIMusahating katindustriHalal/Artic le (Accessed 27 April 2013).

Yemisi, A. B. (2001). The supply chain role of third-party logistics providers. *The International Journal of Logistics Management*, 12(2), 87–102. http://dx.doi.org/10.1108/09574090110806316

Yusaini, H. M., Abd Rahman, A. R., Azanizawati, M., & Mohd Ghazli, H. (2016). Halal traceability in enhancing halal integrity for food industry in Malaysia: A review. *International Research Journal of Engineering and Technology*, 3(3), 68–74.

Zailani, S., Arrifin, Z., Abd Wahid, N., Othman, R., & Fernando, Y. (2010). Halal traceability and halal tracking systems in strengthening halal food supply chain for food industry in Malaysia (A review). *Journal of Food Technology*, 8(3), 74–81.

Zailani, S., Iranmanesh, M., Aziz, A. A., & Kanapathy, K. (2017). Halal logistics opportunities and challenges. *Journal of Islamic Marketing*, 8(1), 127–139. https://doi.org/10.1108/JIMA-04-2015–0028

Zailani, S., Jafarzadeh, S., Iranmanesh, M., Nikbin, D., & Selim, N. I. I. (2018). Halal logistics service quality: Conceptual model and empirical evidence. *British Food Journal*, 120(11), 2599–2614. https://doi.org/10.1108/BFJ-07-2017-0412

Zakaria, N., & Abdul-Talib, S. N. (2010). Applying islamic maket-ortiented cultural model to sensitize strategies towards global customers, competitors, and environment. *Journal of Islamic Marketing*, 1(1), 51–62.

Zakaria, Z. (2008). Tapping into the world Halal market: Some discussions on Malaysian laws and standards. *Shariah Journal*, 16, 603–616.

Zulfakar, M. H. (2013). Australia's halal meat supply chain (AHMSC) operations: Supply chain structure, influencing factors and issues, PhD Thesis, RMIT University.

Zulfakar, M. H., Anuar, M. M., & Talib, M. S. A. (2014). Conceptual framework on halal food supply chain integrity enhancement. *Procedia – Social and Behavioral Sciences*, 121, 58–67. https://doi.org/10.1016/j.sbspro.2014.01.1108

Zulfakar, M. H., Chan, C., & Jie, F. (2014). Factor influencing the operations of Halal meat supply chain in Australia. In Proceeding of the 19th International Symposium on Logistics (ISL2014), Ho Chi Minh City, 6–9 July 2014, pp. 667–674.

Zulfakar, M. H., Jie, F., & Chan, C. (2012). Halal food supply chain integrity: From a literature review to a conceptual framework. In Proceeding of the 10th ANZAM Operations, Supply Chain and service management, Melbourne, 14–15 June 2012, pp. 1–23.

Zulfakar, M. H., Jie, F., & Chan, C. (2013). Critical success factors for a successful implementation of Halal red meat supply chain in Australia: Meat processor's perspective'. In Proceeding of the 27th Australian and New Zealand Academy of Management (ANZAM 2013) conference, Hobart, Tasmania, 4–6 December 2013, p. 115.

Index

Note: **Bold** page numbers refer to tables and *italic* page numbers refer to figures.

Printed in the United States
by Baker & Taylor Publisher Services

Printed in the United States
by Baker & Taylor Publisher Services